BARRON'S DOG BIBLES

Bichon Frise

Richard G. Beauchamp

Acknowledgments

I met my first Bichon Frise in 1969 at a rare breed dog show and the breed has been a part of my life ever since. I can't help but marvel at how incredibly well it has done in little more than 30 years since its recognition by the American Kennel Club. The Bichon was literally unknown in the beginning of the 1970s but by 2001, a member of the breed went on to score Best in Show at Westminster Kennel Club, dogdom's "show of shows." There is no doubt whatsoever that hard work and dedication on the part of the Bichon Frise's diehard fanciers played a significant role in the breed's meteoric rise to prominence in such a short time. However, having outlets to disseminate sound and realistic information for and about the breed cannot be underestimated as a good part of the reason for the breed's success. Barron's Educational Series has been significant in allowing us to accomplish this. Had it not been for the enthusiastic support at Barron's Educational Series over the years, I seriously doubt the Bichon Frise would have been so readily accepted in the hearts and minds of dog lovers everywhere. I feel certain the readers of this book will find a great deal within its pages to help make living with a Bichon a joyful, long-term relationship for both dog and owner.

I particularly want to thank my editor, Angela Tartaro, who has assisted me so well in consolidating all the bits and pieces of my experiences with Bichons into this book. There are always so many loose ends to be connected in the final stages of producing any book and Angela has been incredibly helpful in my being able to do so.

About the Author

Richard G. (Rick) Beauchamp has been actively involved with the Bichon Frise breed since its earliest days in America. Under his Beau Monde kennel breed prefix he has bred upwards of 100 champion Bichons, many of them Best in Show winners here and abroad. He has also bred champions in many other breeds, including American Cocker Spaniels, Boxers, Doberman Pinschers, Wire Fox Terriers, Chinese Shar-Pei, and Poodle. The influence of his outstanding dogs extends itself beyond the United States to many other countries of the world. Rick participated in writing the current American Kennel Club standard of the Bichon Frise. He is an AKC judge and has judged purebred dogs in every major country of the world, including the Bichon Frise breed at the 2004 Crufts show in England—the world's largest dog show. He has written books on over 50 different dog breeds and is a regular columnist for *Dogs in Review*, *Dog World*, and South Africa's *All About Dogs* magazines. He also frequently lectures on breeding and judging.

All information and advice contained in this book has been reviewed by a veterinarian.

A Word About Pronouns

Many dog lovers feel that the pronoun "it" is not appropriate when referring to a pet that can be such a wonderful part of our lives. For this reason, Bichon Frise's are referred to as "Pierre" or "he" throughout this book unless the topic specifically relates to female dogs. This by no means infers any preference, nor should it be taken as an indication that either sex is particularly problematic.

Photo Credits

Tara Darling: i, iii, 3, 5, 11, 12, 14, 19, 20, 24, 29, 51, 53, 61, 63, 65, 68, 71, 72, 78, 92, 100, 123, 140, 145, 146, 150; Cheryl A. Ertelt: 49, 80, 106; Isabelle Francais: 8, 39, 46, 52, 66, 118, 122, 133; Gressick: 121, 125; Karen Hudson: 143; Daniel Johnson/Paulette Johnson 111–115; Paulette Johnson: iv, 16, 18, 22, 23, 26, 32, 44, 54, 56, 59, 76, 86, 91, 94, 96, 99, 110, 116, 130, 134, 135, 136, 139, 154; Pets by Paulette: 10, 36, 75; Shutterstock: 7, 88, 105; Toni Tucker: 127, 128, 129

Cover Credits

Tara Darling: front and back cover.

All inquiries should be addressed to:
Barron's Educational Series, Inc.
250 Wireless Boulevard
Hauppauge, New York 11788
www.barronseduc.com

ISBN-13 (book): 978-0-7641-6229-9
ISBN-10 (book): 0-7641-6229-2
ISBN-13 (DVD): 978-0-7641-8678-3
ISBN-10 (DVD): 0-7641-8678-7
ISBN-13 (package): 978-0-7641-9625-6
ISBN-10 (package): 0-7641-9625-1

Library of Congress Catalog Card No.: 2008036384

Library of Congress Cataloging-in-Publication Data

Beauchamp, Richard G.
Bichon frise / by Richard G. Beauchamp.
p. cm.— (Barron's dog bibles)
Includes bibliographical references and index.
ISBN-13: 978-0-7641-6229-9 (alk. paper)
ISBN-10: 0-7641-6229-2 (alk. paper)
ISBN-13: 978-0-7641-8678-3 (alk. paper)
ISBN-10: 0-7641-8678-7 (alk. paper)
1. Bichon frise. I. Title.

SF429.B52B425 2009
636.72—dc22

2008036384

Printed in China

9 8 7 6 5 4 3 2

CONTENTS

CONTENTS

PREFACE

The Bichon Frise (pronounced Bee-*shon* Fri-*zay)* is more often than not simply referred to by the breed's shortened name—Bichon. For the purpose of this book you will most often find him referred to as "Pierre," a name I find very suitable considering the breed's close association with the castles and the streets of France. The Bichon is indeed a unique little breed that has a very long and very challenging history.

He's weathered the ups and downs of world politics and withstood the fickle nature of the various classes of society that have taken him in and out of favor. He has shared the trappings of royalty and endured the rugged life of the sailors who transported him to ports around the world. A good part of his history has been spent as a pampered darling on the laps of the ladies of the court and just as much of it as a street urchin helping peddlers and organ grinders eke out their meager living.

Ever resilient, the Bichon has sprung back from where the fates have taken him with a constitution not diminished by its challenges but actually made stronger. Beneath the white teddy bear of a coat beats the heart of a true survivor.

An indestructible nature and appealing looks make the Bichon a most desirable companion, but no breed is "the breed for everyone," and certainly not the Bichon Frise—he takes patience and a lot of care. This is not the dog for someone who would like a little hothouse flower that needs attention only when the owner has the time to spare it.

In order for the Bichon to develop into the charming little dog the breed can be his owner must be prepared to give him all the attention he deserves and all the guidance he needs. The Bichon whose owner has neglected his dog's training is nothing but a nuisance.

This book introduces both the joys and drawbacks of owning this delightful breed and provides the information you need to understand your Bichon Frise and his innate behaviors. What follows on these pages is the attempt of a longtime breeder and owner to share all those things that will help you give your Bichon the best of care and help him develop into the wonderful little dog he was bred to be.

Richard G. Beauchamp

Chapter One

All About the Bichon Frise

Some of you who are reading this book may just be in the thinking stage of whether or not you want to become the owner of a Bichon Frise. On the other hand, your own personal "Pierre" may be sitting there at your feet as you read this. Possibly you have done all the research—visited kennels or homes of people who live with Bichons and you're convinced that the Bichon is the dog for you.

The information presented in this chapter might at first reading appear a bit too elementary for the level of decision-making that you have yet to do in regard to the breed, but it is the basic stuff—the information that can only serve to enhance your relationship with your Bichon. And then, too, as an old mentor of mine once told me, "No one knows what they don't know!"

Knowing how dogs got here in the first place can teach you a great deal about why your very civilized Bichon does things that seem totally out of character. It will also help you understand why some doggie behavior is very hard, if not practically impossible, to alter.

Why is this important? If you plan to live with a dog of any breed, above all, you and the dog must find life more than just tolerable. In order for a dog to be a sound and stable representative of its breed, the dog has to be raised in an environment conducive to achieving his genetic potential. So, let's begin at the very beginning and see how Pierre wound up sitting on your sofa or will be sitting there just as soon as you can arrange it to be so.

All dogs, from the tiniest toy breed up to the most massive of the working breeds have one common ancestor—the wolf. As hard as it may be to imagine, your Bichon's heritage traces back to the same ancestors as those of your next-door neighbor's hunting dog and the Rottweiler down the street. The story of how the wolf evolved into man's best friend began well over ten thousand years ago in the dawning of history's Mesolithic period.

The braver members of the wolf packs that existed in those early days found an easy source of food in the discards around human campsites. Eventually the wolves and the humans who lived in the campsites became accustomed to seeing each other and the more human-friendly of the wolves took up residence ever more closely to human dwellings. This took the wolves one step further along the path to domestication.

FYI: Innate Behaviors

Hundreds, sometimes thousands, of years have been invested in shaping the manner in which breeds look, react, and behave. But there are behaviors that are even more firmly fixed than those imposed by humans—the things that were passed down from the very source, thousands of years ago. Trying to change the basic character of your Bichon, particularly in many of the instinctive behavioral areas, can only result in a difficult situation for both you and your dog, creating an imperfect match. Time has proven dogs that go into the wrong homes do not remain there and, all too often, wind up in animal shelters or on the streets!

As centuries passed, wolves evolved into four separate and distinct branches or races: *Canis lupus*, the rugged northern gray wolf, *Canis lupus pallipes*, an Asian wolf; *Canis lupus chanco* or *laniger*, the wooly coated wolf of Tibet and Northern India; and *Canis lupus arabs*, a small desert wolf of Arabia. Each of these branches developed separate skills and modifications in appearance, as well as subtly different temperamental and behavioral traits. The great diversity in dogs that were to follow began with these wolf groups. Even the dogs who remained of a strain relatively uninfluenced by crosses to other wolf groups would later lose their "purity" in the hands of man, who found both desirable and undesirable characteristics existing across the groups and intentionally manipulated the gene pools to both intensify and eliminate specific traits.

It's important to understand that all this was not a single isolated incident, but something that went on in many different parts of the world with different kinds of people and different branches of the wolf family. Further, although it seems like it might have been happening simultaneously over a few hundred years, it was actually occurring at different rates and times spread out over thousands of years.

The road from wolf-in-the-wild, *Canis lupus*, to "man's best friend," *Canis familiaris*, or dog, is long and fascinating, as it is accompanied by widely varying explanations. There are some things, however, that historians generally seem to agree on: Wolves were employed to assist man in acquiring food, and certain descendants of these increasingly domesticated wolves could also be used by man to assist in survival pursuits other than hunting.

Canine historians Richard and Alice Feinnes' book *The Natural History of Dogs*, is an interesting and enlightening study of the development of dog breeds. In it they classify most dogs as having descended from one of four major groups: the Dingo Group, the Greyhound Group, the Arctic or Nordic Group, and the Mastiff Group. Each of these groups trace back to separate and distinct branches of the wolf family.

The Dingo Group traces its origin to the Asian wolf. Two well-known examples of the Dingo Group are the Basenji and, through the mixture of the blood of several European breeds, the Rhodesian Ridgeback.

The Greyhound Group descends from a coursing type relative of the Asian Wolf. The group includes all those dogs that hunt by sight and are capable of great speed. The Greyhound itself, the Afghan Hound, the Borzoi, and Irish Wolfhound are all examples of this group and have become known as the coursing breeds. They are not true Hounds in that they do not use their noses to locate or follow prey.

The Arctic or Nordic Group of dogs is a direct descendent of the rugged northern wolf also known as the Gray Wolf. Included in the many breeds of this group are the Alaskan Malamute, the Chow Chow, the German Shepherd, and the much smaller Welsh Corgi and Spitz type dog.

The fourth classification is the Mastiff Group, which owes its primary heritage to the Tibetan wolf. The great diversity of the dogs included in this group indicates that they are not entirely of pure blood in that the specific breeds included have undoubtedly been influenced by descendants of the other three groups.

Current archeological discoveries indicate that there were at least several different humanoid types in existence as civilization developed; however, village people, being smarter and more experienced than their cave-dwelling ancestors and counterparts, realized through selection that they could customize the wolves to suit more specific needs. Humans were realizing what the wolf descendants *looked like* also had a great bearing on what they could accomplish.

About this time in history we stop calling the animals we are talking about wolves, and start referring to them as *Canis familiaris*—dogs.

So much for 12,000 years of history. The important point to remember in all this is that the wolf brought a whole set of characteristics to their dog descendants that took mankind thousands of years to modify. Succeeding generations were carefully manipulated by close breeding, weeding out undesirable characteristics and intensifying desirable traits. It took the best part of 13 millennia of natural transition and intentional selectivity to reach the level some of our purebred breeds stand at today.

As humans grew more sophisticated they began to observe the fact that certain of these wolf descendants were more helpful in some areas than they were in others. For example, some were better at hunting, others quicker to sound the alarm when intruders appeared. Selecting from the more adept in these respects were man's first attempts at breeding dogs for specific duties. Later, as campsites grew into towns and cities and the leisure classes developed, so did a desire for small attractive dogs that had little purpose other than companionship.

Fun Facts

Documentation of controlled breeding of dogs can be found as early as the first century A.D. when the Romans had classified dogs into general groups: guard dogs, shepherd's dogs, fighting or war dogs, and hunting dogs. The hunting dogs were of two classifications—those that hunted by sight and others who hunted by scent.

Many breeds can be traced directly back to members of these early groups. Combining individuals from two or more of these different categories to create yet another breed developed even more breeds.

A Brief History

The companion dogs we are primarily interested in here are those that created the Bichon family. This new family was the result of combining the blood of a medium-sized water spaniel type dog known as the Barbet and a simultaneously existing family of light-colored, small lap or ladies' dogs that are thought to have originated in the Far East.

From this combination a small, often white, breed of dog evolved. Known as the Small Barbet or Barbichon (later shortened simply to Bichon), these little white dogs existed throughout the area surrounding the Mediterranean Sea at the time before Christ. The combination that produced the Barbichon also proved to be the basis for a number of other small companion breeds, including the Maltese and the Poodle.

Because they were small enough, these companion dogs often traveled with their owners, some of whom were seamen. These rough and tumble sailors fancied the Bichon's small size, hardiness, and amiable disposition and took the little dogs along as reminders of the homes they would not see for many months at a time.

These sailors quickly found that their little Bichons not only had value as trade, they also had great appeal among the ladies in the foreign ports that were visited. Before long, young ladies in lands as far off as the Philippines,

FYI: The Bichon Frise in Art

Through the centuries works of art have included small white dogs that could be easily identified as precursors to the Bichon Frise and other breeds in the Bichon family. *The Lady and the Unicorn*, said to have been woven by Albrecht Durer at the end of the fifteenth century, includes a distinctly Bichon-type dog.

The most famous work of art picturing a Bichon Frise is the late sixteenth-century portrait of the Duchess of Alba by Francisco Goya. In an oil on canvas painted by Emile Carolus-Duran in 1874, the small white dog accompanying Marie Anne Carulus-Duran would easily be recognized as a Bichon Frise.

In 1988, U.S. Bichon Frise breeder and exhibitor Lois Morrow acquired a seventeenth-century painting by Henrietta Ronner-Knip entitled *A Bichon*. The Bichon in the Ronner-Knip painting bears a striking resemblance to the dog in the Carolus-Duran art piece. Undoubtedly the Bichon Frise was well on his way to establishing himself as a legitimate breed earlier than written records indicate.

Cuba, Argentina, and Tenerife were waving goodbye to their seafaring lovers with tears in their eyes and Bichons in their arms.

These little dogs became established and flourished in their new homes, developing into several distinct varieties. These were to become known as the Bichon Maltaise, the Bichon Bolognese, the Bichon Havanese, and the Bichon Tenerife. The latter is chiefly credited as the forerunner of today's Bichon Frise. However, as we will see, the similar origin of all Bichons, their subsequent interrelated histories, and their physical similarities make crediting the dog from Tenerife as the Bichon Frise's only ancestor a dubious distinction. Problems that modern breeders encounter in maintaining the Bichon's desired "look" constantly recall what might be considered obvious characteristics of their close relatives.

The Canary and Tenerife islands are considered the developmental centers of the breed that was known for many years as the Bichon Tenerife, and later as the Bichon Frise. It can only be assumed the indigenous breeds of the new lands crossed with the Bichon type dogs left behind by travelers. These crosses obviously flourished and generations later their descendants made their way full circle back to both Spain and Italy.

Little appears in French literature about the Tenerife dog after the 1500s until the rise of Napoleon III (nephew of Napoleon Bonaparte) into power in the middle years of the nineteenth century. The Bichon Tenerife is frequently mentioned in French literature during that century and is frequently portrayed with members of the royal courts in the works of leading artists of the period.

Fun Facts

During the 1500s the French were highly influenced by Italy's Renaissance and it was very fashionable in France to adopt everything Italian. Part of the fashion trend in the French courts was Italy's little white Bichon Tenerife. Francis I, patron of the Renaissance (1515–1547 A.D.) was particularly fond of the breed during his reign.

By the end of the nineteenth century the Bichon was replaced in the favor of the court by other breeds, but hardy as he was, the Bichon Tenerife survived and would more often than not be found in the streets of Paris and other cities accompanying tradesmen and street musicians. The nimble Bichons were highly trainable and loved to perform for the crowds. The breed demonstrated a unique ability to walk on their hind legs for long distances and usually did so while pawing the air. Passersby interpreted the trick as begging for money and often responded by opening their purses.

Europe's great circuses and carnivals also took advantage of the Bichon's extroverted personalities and uncanny ability to learn and perform tricks. The dogs were undoubtedly bred and the offspring selected with the ability to entertain foremost in mind. To this day the breed retains their entertaining capabilities and Bichon owners are amazed to find their dogs walking on their hind legs, performing somersaults and other feats of dexterity with no training whatsoever.

The Bichon Frise Gets His Name

Reduced to minimal numbers by the end of World War I, Bichons escaped extinction only through the efforts of a few valiant fanciers who gathered what remained of the breed from the streets of France and Belgium. Working cooperatively, those who found pleasure in the happy little dogs were able to obtain breed recognition under the auspices of the Societe Centrale Canine in March of 1933. The breed was officially given the name "Bichon à Poil Frise," which translates as "Bichon of the curly hair."

Just when it looked as though devotees had secured the future of the Bichon Frise, another Great War threatened the newly named breed. Here, again, the breed's hardiness and the determination of their owners assisted the Bichon Frise through this devastating ordeal.

There can be little doubt that the checkered history of the Bichon Frise through the centuries included liaisons with his three cousins: the Bichon Maltaise, Bolognese, and Havanese. The breed was classified and legitimized as a pure and distinct breed by the French in 1933, but what remained of the

breed in Europe after the close of World War II was most likely a conglomerate of the several Bichon varieties.

Bichons Set Sail for America

In 1952 Helene and Francois Picault of Deippe, France became interested in the breed. They exhibited briefly in France, and eventually emigrated to America, where they optimistically anticipated making a fortune through the sale of their little white dogs.

But alas, the "fortune" never materialized for the Picaults. Their family of Bichons grew rapidly, but sales of animals not registered with the American Kennel Club (AKC) were hard to carry out regardless of the breed's charm. In the early 1960s a few individuals acquired stock from the Picaults, while others, completely unaware of the Picaults presence in the U.S., returned from travels to France and Belgium with a Bichon or two tucked under their arms.

The "New" Bichon

Interest in this "new" breed began to develop gradually. Thanks to the efforts of the Bichon's devoted followers, the AKC accepted the Bichon Frise into its Miscellaneous Class competition in September of 1971. This class was, and still is, one of the first steps a new breed takes on its way to full recognition by the AKC.

In the following two years, the breed attracted greater attention and had such universal acceptance by dog fanciers that it was hard to believe that they were not a fully-accredited AKC breed. Finally, late in 1972 it was announced that the AKC had granted the Bichon Frise full recognition.

The Bichon Frise Breed Standard

There is no doubt about it; the Bichon Frise has great eye appeal. His teddy bear coat combined with a jet black nose and twinkling dark eyes have attracted thousands of owners not only here in the U.S. but throughout the world.

Bichon Frise Characteristics

The good looks and sparkling personality of the Bichon Frise are no accident. The breed comes by all its appealing characteristics through decades of concentrated effort by dedicated breeders who have judiciously selected stock capable of reproducing the mental and physical qualities that best define the breed. All of these qualities are outlined in the Bichon Frise's official breed standard.

Familiarizing yourself with the Bichon's anatomy will make it much easier to explain any problems your dog may encounter to your veterinarian or breeder. Using precise terminology is far more likely to enable them to offer advice over the phone or in conversation.

There is a great deal more to the Bichon Frise than what the breed looks like. In Chapter 2 we will take a look at the breed's all-important personality and compatibility characteristics that should be given strong consideration prior to bringing a Bichon into your life.

Official American Kennel Club Standard of the Bichon Frise

General Appearance The Bichon Frise is a small, sturdy, white powder puff of a dog whose merry temperament is evidenced by his plumed tail carried jauntily over the back and his dark-eyed inquisitive expression.

This is a breed that has no gross or incapacitating exaggerations and therefore there is no inherent reason for lack of balance or unsound movement.

Any deviation from the ideal described in the standard should be penalized to the extent of the deviation. Structural faults common to all breeds are as undesirable in the Bichon Frise as in any other breed, even though such faults may not be specifically mentioned in the standard.

Size Dogs and bitches 9½ to 11½ inches are to be given primary preference. Only where the comparative superiority of a specimen outside this range clearly justifies it should greater latitude be taken. In no case, however, should this latitude ever extend over 12 inches or under 9 inches. The minimum limits do not apply to puppies. *Proportion*—The body from the forward-most point of the chest to the point of rump is ¼ longer than the height at the withers. The body from the withers to lowest point of chest represents ½ the distance from withers to ground. *Substance*—Compact and of medium bone throughout; neither coarse nor fine.

Head *Expression*—Soft, dark-eyed, inquisitive, alert. *Eyes* are round, black or dark brown and are set in the skull to look directly forward. An overly large or bulging eye is a fault as is an almond shaped, obliquely set eye. Halos, the black or very dark brown skin surrounding the eyes, are necessary as they accentuate the eye and enhance expression. The eye rims themselves must be black. Broken pigment, or total absence of pigment on the eye rims produce a blank and staring expression, which is a definite fault. Eyes of any color other than black or dark brown are a very serious fault and must be severely penalized. *Ears* are drop and are covered with long flowing hair. When extended toward the nose, the leathers reach approximately halfway the length of the muzzle. They are

Breed Truths

The History Makers

The first Bichon Frise to complete an American championship was Charles and Dolores Wolskie's C & D Count Kristopher.

The first all-breed Best in Show to be won by a Bichon took place at Farmington Valley Kennel Club on July 7, 1973. Mr. Louis Murr selected Mrs. William Tabler's Ch. Chaminade Syncopation for the award, just three short months after the breed had gained AKC recognition. The handler was Ted Young, Jr.

The first winner of the Bichon Frise Club of America's National Specialty show was Mrs. Nan Busk's Ch. Vogelflight's Music Man. Judge Langdon Skarda presented the award, in June of 1976. The handler was Joe Waterman.

The first Bichon to win Best in Show, All Breeds at Westminster Kennel Club was Ch. Special Times Just Right, owned by Cecelia Ruggles, Eleanor McDonald, and Flavio Werneck. The date was February 14, 2001. The Judge was Dorothy M. Macdonald, and the handler was Scott Sommer.

set on slightly higher than eye level and rather forward on the skull, so that when the dog is alert they serve to frame the face. The ***skull*** is slightly rounded, allowing for a round and forward looking eye. The ***stop*** is slightly accentuated. *Muzzle*—A properly balanced head is three parts muzzle to five parts skull, measured from the nose to the stop and from the stop to the occiput. A line drawn between the outside corners of the eyes and to the nose will create a near equilateral triangle. There is a slight degree of chiseling under the eyes, but not so much as to result in a weak or snipey foreface. The lower jaw is strong. The ***nose*** is prominent and always black. ***Lips*** are black, fine, never drooping. ***Bite*** is scissors. A bite which is undershot or overshot should be severely penalized. A crooked or out of line tooth is permissible; however, missing teeth are to be severely faulted.

Neck, Topline, and Body The arched ***neck*** is long and carried proudly behind an erect head. It blends smoothly into the shoulders. The length of neck from occiput to withers is approximately ⅓ the distance from forechest to buttocks. The ***topline*** is level except for a slight, muscular arch over the loin. *Body*—The chest is well developed and wide enough to allow free and unrestricted movement of the front legs. The lowest point of the chest extends at least to the elbow. The rib cage is moderately sprung and extends back to a short and muscular loin. The forechest is well pronounced and protrudes slightly forward of the point of shoulder. The underline has a moderate tuck-up. ***Tail*** is well plumed, set on level with the topline and curved gracefully over the back so that the hair of the tail rests on the back. When the tail is extended toward the head it reaches at least halfway to the withers. A low tail set, a tail carried perpendicularly to the back, or a tail which droops behind is to be severely penalized. A corkscrew tail is a very serious fault.

Forequarters *Shoulders*—The shoulder blade, upper arm and forearm are approximately equal in length. The shoulders are laid back to somewhat near a forty-five degree angle. The upper arm extends well back so the elbow is placed directly below the withers when viewed from the side. ***Legs*** are of medium bone; straight, with no bow or curve in the forearm or wrist. The elbows are held close to the body. The ***pasterns*** slope slightly from the vertical. The dewclaws may be removed. The ***feet*** are tight and round, resembling those of a cat and point directly forward, turning neither in nor out. ***Pads*** are black. Nails are kept short.

Hindquarters The hindquarters are of medium bone, well angulated with muscular thighs and spaced moderately wide. The upper and lower thigh are nearly equal in length meeting at a well bent stifle joint. The leg from hock joint to foot pad is perpendicular to the ground. Dewclaws may be removed. Paws are tight and round with black pads.

Coat The texture of the coat is of utmost importance. The undercoat is soft and dense, the outer coat of a coarser and curlier texture. The combination of the two gives a soft but substantial feel to the touch which is similar to plush or velvet and when patted springs back. When bathed and brushed, it stands off the body, creating an overall powder puff appearance. A wiry coat is not desirable. A limp, silky coat, a coat that lies down, or a lack of undercoat are very serious faults. ***Trimming***—The coat is trimmed to reveal the natural outline of the body. It is rounded off from any direction and never cut so short as to create an overly trimmed or squared off appearance. The furnishings of the head, beard, mustache, ears and tail are left longer. The longer head hair is trimmed to create an overall rounded impression. The topline is trimmed to appear level. The coat is long enough to maintain the powder puff look which is characteristic of the breed.

Color Color is white, may have shadings of buff, cream or apricot around the ears or on the body. Any color in excess of 10% of the entire coat of a mature specimen is a fault and should be penalized, but color of the accepted shadings should not be faulted in puppies.

Gait Movement at a trot is free, precise and effortless. In profile the forelegs and hind legs extend equally with an easy reach and drive that maintain a steady topline. When moving, the head and neck remain somewhat erect and as speed increases there is a very slight convergence of legs toward the center line. Moving away, the hindquarters travel with moderate width between them and the foot pads can be seen. Coming and going, his movement is precise and true.

Temperament Gentle mannered, sensitive, playful and affectionate. A cheerful attitude is the hallmark of the breed and one should settle for nothing less.

The Importance of Breed Standards

Before the breed is given official recognition, the sponsoring breed club is also required to submit a written description of the breed that gives a word picture of both what the breed should look like and how it should interact with humans. This written description is called the *breed standard*.

The presiding kennel club of each country of the world has a registering system for the purebred dogs that are born and bred in their respective countries. (The AKC is the chief recognized authority here in the United States.) These registering systems issue certificates of registration that are probably best described as canine birth certificates. These birth, or more properly "registration," certificates are just as important as ours. The only way a Bichon Frise can be considered a "purebred" and be "registered" is if the Bichon's father and mother (*sire* and *dam* in dog parlance) are registered, and the only way the sire and dam can be registered is if their parents were registered, and so on.

In order for a breed to be accepted by one of the registering sources in the first place, the supporters of the breed (in this case the Bichon Frise Club of America [BFCA]) have to provide credentials certifying their dogs have been bred true to form and free of outcrosses (introduction of other breeds into the gene pool) for at least five generations. This is a relatively simple task for the BFCA, in that all Bichons born in or imported into the United States were descendants of dogs that were registered with AKC-recognized European countries.

Fun Facts

A breed standard is a detailed description of an individual breed meant to portray the *ideal* specimen of that breed. This includes ideal structure, temperament, gait, and type—all aspects of the dog. Because the standard describes an ideal specimen, it isn't based on any particular dog. It is a concept against which judges compare actual dogs at dog shows and which breeders strive to produce in their breeding programs. At a dog show, the dog that wins is the one that comes closest, in the judge's opinion, to the standard for its breed. Breed standards are written by the breed parent clubs. These clubs are the national organizations formed to oversee the well-being of the breed. The standards are voted on and approved by the members of the parent clubs.

In most cases, original breed standards were written by the people responsible for creating the breed or by people who were personally familiar with the breed's origin, purpose, and development over the years. Necessary revisions that take place through time are usually made by members of the national breed organizations formed to oversee the well-being of the breed.

10 Questions Most Asked About the Bichon Frise

1 **Is the Bichon a cross between the Poodle and the Maltese?** The Bichon, the Maltese, the Toy Poodle, and the old but newly popular Havanese are basically all descendants of a small white dog that is said to have existed around the Mediterranean Sea since before the time of Christ. The four breeds are all, in effect, "cousins" rather than one being a descendant of or a "cross" with another. The Bichon Frise was a purebred breed of its own for several centuries but became an "official" breed with the Fédération Cynologique Internationale (FCI) when the Société Centrale Canine in France gave the breed its name, "Bichon à Poil Frise" in 1933.

2 **How popular are Bichons in the United States?** There are currently over 160 breeds recognized by the AKC. At this writing, the Bichon Frise ranks in the low 30s in annual registrations, a position that it has generally maintained for the past decade. True Bichon fanciers make no attempts to gain great popularity for the breed, in that over the years, extreme popularity of other breeds has served only to have a negative effect.

3 **Why do some Bichons have short legs and long bodies while others seem more long-legged?** Dwarfed legs and long bodies are faulty recessives that lurk in the Bichon Frise breed's gene pool. Despite the fact that educated breeders make every effort to eliminate the problem from their bloodline, the dwarf-type of Bichon still continues to crop up from time to time. Although healthy in most other respects, these dwarfed individuals are usually sold with a neutering proviso.

4 **Is the Bichon Frise really a French breed?** Although the breed originally emanated from the area around the Mediterranean, it was France and Belgium that actually "legitimatized" the Bichon by accepting the breed into their registries. Technically, the two countries are countries of development, but most often are also given credit as countries of origin.

5 **How can I tell if my Bichon is good enough to show?** If you are unable to contact the person who actually bred the litter that your puppy came from, the best way to determine the dog's show potential is to contact an active breeder who has produced champions in the breed. This is best done when a Bichon is six months old or older. Before that age, the most any experienced person in the breed would venture to say of a puppy is that it does or does not have show *potential*.

6 **How old will my Bichon live to be?** It is impossible to accurately predict how old any breed of dog might live to be, but generally speaking, the Bichon Frise is a relatively long-lived breed. Proper care, which includes correct nutrition and sufficient exercise certainly enhances the chances that a Bichon can easily live a happy life to his 12th or 14th birthday. There are numerous cases in which Bichons have lived well beyond even that advanced age.

7 **How can I tell if my Bichon is good enough to breed?** If a Bichon is purchased from a respected breeder, that question will already have been answered. Established breeders know at an early age which of the puppies they produce should be used for breeding and which should not. In fact, today's breeders will almost always sell a puppy that they do not want to see bred with what is called a "limited registration." A puppy with that stipulation on his or her registration certificate can neither be shown in conformation shows nor ever have puppies that can be registered. Should a Bichon come from a situation in which this was not handled initially, it is, again, best to contact a reliable breeder, to seek his opinion as to whether the dog is good enough to breed.

8 **Is it hard to housetrain a Bichon?** Some breeds seem to be born housetrained. Bichons are not one of those breeds—they forget! That said, if the trainer is absolutely, positively dedicated to the task, it can be done in a reasonable length of time. Avoidance is the key word here, however. Think of it this way—for every time you allow an accident to occur, your housetraining time is extended yet another month. The bottom line has to be keeping a constant eye on your little Bichon when he is not confined to his crate or outdoors.

9 **How can I tell if my Bichon has hip dysplasia?** Hip dysplasia (a degenerative joint disease that results from the abnormal development of the joint that forms the hip) occurs in varying degrees. The canine hip joint is a "ball and socket" joint. The condition of a shallow hip joint and a poorly fitting head of the femur (thigh bone) make the joint unstable to a greater or lesser degree. Some cases are so mild they require X-ray technology to detect that that no symptoms are observable. The condition can progress, however, and lameness can occur, sometimes to the point where it is painful for the dog to use his hindquarters at all. If the condition is suspected, the problem should be discussed with the dog's veterinarian to see if X-rays are advised.

10 **How many times a year should a Bichon be shaved?** The Bichon or any coated dog for that matter should never be shaved unless the coat has become so neglected and matted that there is no other alternative. A Bichon's coat serves as insulation against both heat and cold. Shaving does absolutely nothing to relieve a dog's discomfort during hot summer months. In fact it may well prove to make the dog even more uncomfortable.

Chapter Two

The Mind of a Bichon Frise

It's a black-and-white world for your Bichon Frise. This is important for you to remember as you approach your dog's education and attempt to understand his reaction to life in general.

To you, "drop the ball" and "put the ball down" mean exactly the same thing. To your Bichon, though, one command has absolutely nothing to do with the other. He has learned what to do when you say, "drop the ball," and he associates the action with those exact words. "Put the ball down" means nothing to him outside of perhaps recognizing the word "ball" and associating it with that round thing he likes to play with.

It's the words themselves that count and not their meaning. Conceivably you could teach your dog that the words "chocolate sundae" mean he should drop the ball. Once you understand this it will make training, both formal lessons and household rules, vastly more effective.

Your Bichon must also understand that commands must be obeyed *always.* The fact that "come" means he absolutely must come one time and not the other (because you are busy or preoccupied) means that the command really doesn't count. A command should never be given unless you are able to enforce it. Think of it this way—every time you give a command that you do not follow through on you are telling your dog that it is not really a command, only a choice on his part. He is learning a lesson but not the one you are really intending that he learn.

Dealing with Fears

A good many puppies go through a fear-impression stage early on (between eight to ten weeks) and again at around five months. It is impossible to tell what the youngster may develop a fear of—it could be anything from the vacuum cleaner, a flag flapping in the breeze, even a camera, or a particular person.

It is important that these fear situations be handled correctly. Unchecked they last a dog's entire lifetime, seriously affecting his ability to adjust to

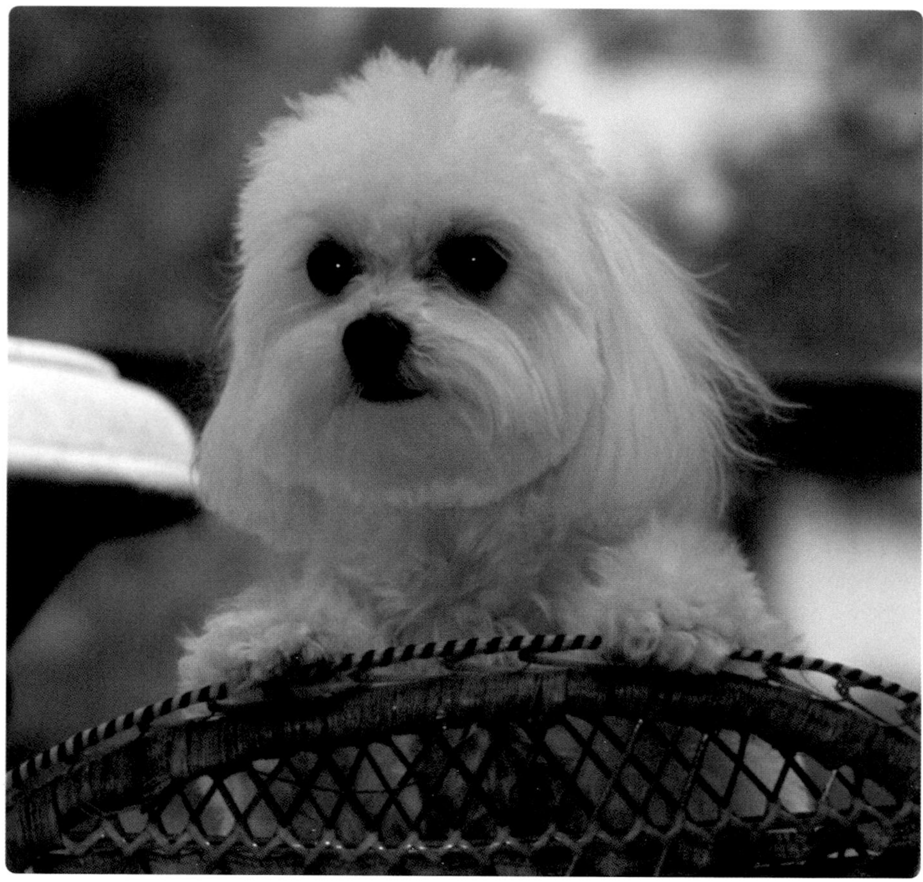

normal situations and they can even lead to fear-biting. When your puppy reacts in fear do not get down and attempt to protect him. Your hovering over him and clutching him to you tells him he should be afraid.

Instead, create situations where he will constantly be introduced to new sounds, people, and unusual situations. It is important that you remain calm and approach the new situation at ease. If it is a stationary object, place toys or treats around it until the puppy becomes confident that the "thing" is not going to harm him.

Separation Issues

The separation blues are a very common problem in dogs left alone. Boredom is often the culprit in the milder cases, and reactions can range in intensity from whimpering to constant barking and howling. Extreme cases can lead to downright neurotic and destructive behavior, such as hysterical barking and destroying furniture. Some dogs go so far as to relieve themselves throughout the home. These more extreme behaviors are usually associated with a somewhat serious condition called separation anxiety.

Howling or barking while the master is gone is best dealt with by using your crate. Place the crate in the same room with you while you are attending to some project that will take a bit of time. Talk to your dog in a calming voice and reassure him that everything is fine.

Begin your absences by walking out of the room for just a minute or so. Increase the time you are gone gradually. When you return, praise the dog in a calm voice or give him a treat. Leaving some article that smells of you will help comfort the dog when you are gone and a Kong toy stuffed with peanut butter will keep your dog's attention on the goodie rather than on your absence.

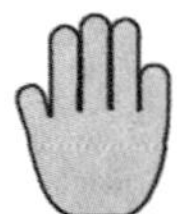

CAUTION

A dog that reacts to loneliness by being destructive should never be allowed to remain loose when you are gone. Some people think it is cruel to confine their dog to an area or his crate where he is not able to destroy things, but they think nothing of becoming furious and frightening the dog out of his wits when he has been free to be destructive. Your reacting in a rage will only tend to enforce the dog's fear of being alone.

Fretting and complaining are reduced considerably if not entirely eliminated when your dog is getting plenty of exercise. A dog with a high level of pent up energy is far more apt to think up things like his dislike of being alone to object to.

Some dogs are fine as long as they can see you. It's your absence that launches the vocal tirade. If your dog or puppy refuses to stay alone without creating major sound effects, begin correcting the behavior by placing the crate in a location where the dog can see you. If the dog begins to whimper to be released, slap your hand down hard on the top of the crate and command, *"Quiet!"*

Nine times out of ten the abrupt noise will startle the dog into at least brief silence. Once he is quiet, praise him for being so good. Doing this once probably won't permanently correct the problem, so you'll have to be adamant about repeating the performance every time your dog lets out even a squeak.

Walk in and out of the room several times and extend your absences gradually. Just as soon as the dog begins to complain, rush back in and repeat the rap on the crate as you give the *Quiet!* command.

PERSONALITY POINTERS

Bichon Frise Body Language

Bichon Frise Mood	Friendly	Curious or Excited	Playful
Head Carriage	Normal posture and head position	Normal posture and head position	"Play bow," chest and head lowered to ground, head looking up
Eyes	Wide open	Wide open	Wide open
Ears	Alert, forward	Alert, forward	Alert, forward
Mouth	Closed or relaxed and slightly open in a "smile"	Mouth open, teeth covered with lips, may pant	Closed or slightly open
Body	Relaxed posture or wiggling with excitement	Relaxed posture or wiggling with excitement	Chest lowered to ground, rump elevated
Tail	Wagging	Wagging	Wagging

The truly stubborn complainers require more drastic measures. Follow the steps above but instead of slapping the crate when your dog complains about your absence, rush back and give the dog a good shot of water from the steady stream cycle of a spray bottle. This method seems very effective with even the most stubborn offender.

Some dogs are fine indoors, but resent being left outdoors. If this is the case, get an empty aluminum soft drink can and drop a small handful of pennies into it. Shaking the can makes a surprisingly loud clatter. When your dog begins to bark, throw the can at the fence or on the ground near the dog. If possible do not let him see you throw the can. Lead him to believe that his noise caused the commotion.

Apprehensive or Anxious	Fearful	Subordinate
Neck stiff, head may be pulled back slightly	Head slightly lowered	Head slightly lowered
Wide open, may appear bug-eyed, whites of eyes may show, may have fixed stare	Eyes wide, whites of eyes may show	Eyes partially closed
Pulled back	Ears pulled back or flattened against skull	Ears flattened against skull
Closed or slightly open in a tight "grin" with teeth showing	Slightly open, teeth may be visible, may be drooling	Lips of mouth pulled back in "grin," may lick or nuzzle
Tense	Tense, trembling, may take on a position poised to run, may release anal sac contents in fear	May roll over on back and expose belly, may also dribble urine in submission
Partially lowered	Lowered, between legs	Lowered, between legs

These treatments are usually very effective. But then again, some dogs are more persistent than others, and it is up to you to be unswerving in your dedication to the task. Above all, you must have the last word. Never release or admit the dog because he is barking or howling. Release can only come when he is doing what you demand, never because he complained long enough or loud enough.

Separation Anxiety

Separation anxiety is a problem of a more serious nature and is the result of a dog's fear of being left alone. It is not spiteful behavior; the dog is simply reacting to his fear in a frenzied manner. This problem is emotionally based and can be a difficult one to correct without assistance. There are new drugs that have been approved to help relieve the high anxiety that separation creates for some dogs. They act on the dog in a manner similar to the calming effect of antidepressants on humans.

These drugs can be obtained by prescription through your veterinarian. Although they do not actually cure the problem, they relieve the symptoms enough so that retraining can begin. And it is the retraining that is the operative word here. Another dog or even a cat, if the two are compatible,

can often solve the anxiety problem immediately, while other dogs respond well to something as simple as having the radio playing while their owners are gone.

Regardless of the cause—loneliness or separation anxiety—owners who make their departures and returns monumental events compound the problem. Don't upset your dog before leaving by giving the poor fellow hugs and kisses as though you are embarking on a yearlong safari. Just go!

When you return, don't make it a climax suitable for the theater screen. Some dogs love those dramatic returns and begin vocally requesting them the minute you walk out the door. Make leaving and coming home as uneventful as possible, or distract your dog by offering him a toy or treat before you leave. If he is happily occupied, the chances are he won't even notice you've gone.

Barking

Not every barking dog is lonely or suffering from a case of separation anxiety. Some dogs bark at simply *everything!* No matter what the dog sees or hears he has to call the world's attention to it and he does so the only way he can—by barking.

This behavior has to be nipped in the bud. It will not improve on its own and will likely get worse as time goes on. A dog barks because he has put himself in charge. Assuming that role he decides he is guarding his home and all the surrounding territory. Your dog has to learn that he is *not* in charge, you are!

Never yell or scream at your barking dog. Your dog will interpret it as barking and he does not understand the "don't do as I do, do as I say" concept.

The bark-at-everything dog is normally one that will also be quiet when there is nothing to bark at. That is, if confined to his crate or a room that he can't see the outdoors from, he is apt to be quiet unless he hears a strange noise that could set him off.

Basically the remedy here is much the same as that employed for separation blues and separation anxiety: teach your dog that he cannot bark at will. Block off the vantage points he has to the outdoors, such as low windows or furniture that gives him access to the higher windows.

The quick-to-bark dog should not be left outdoors alone for long periods of time. If a dog has any territorial instinct at all, he will bark to sound the alarm when he sees or hears something that is out of the ordinary.

The ball is entirely in your court on this one. You have to be there to say *"No!"* and enforce the *no!* command in *every* instance. It's all about putting yourself in charge and leaving no doubt in Pierre's mind that you are the boss and that what you say goes.

Bichons and Obedience

Everything about the Bichon's personality indicates they are a nonaggressive breed. Generally speaking the breed is somewhat submissive. We have never seen a Bichon even indicate that he would challenge his owner on any point regardless of how much he might object to what he is being asked to do.

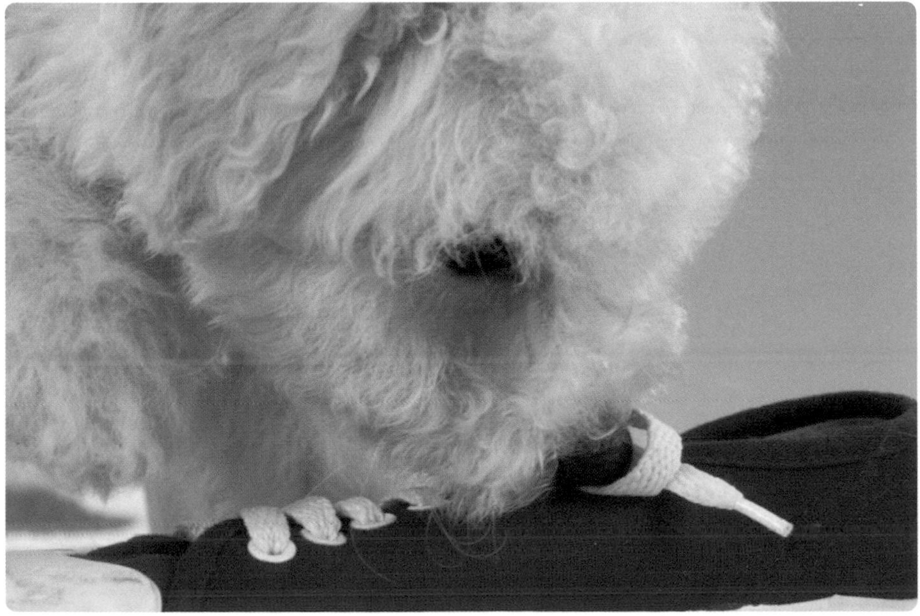

FYI: The Bichon Temperament

Never select a puppy that appears suspicious or runs in fear. All Bichon puppies should have sunny, amiable temperaments. If your puppy had a sunny disposition growing up but has started showing aggressive tendencies at maturity, it is more apt to indicate lack of proper training. Again, only one of you can be in charge. If your dog realizes he can behave as he chooses and has any inclination toward aggressiveness, you have a difficult situation on your hands. Proper training and the establishment of definite boundaries will help to control this type of aggressive behavior. Absolutely no law-abiding citizen should have to endure being menaced by an aggressive dog of any size. The size of the Bichon does not lessen the degree of fear experienced by those who have a fear of dogs. To them Pierre biting at their ankles is no less terrifying than an attack-trained dog of a large breed threatening to do them harm.

A stern tone of voice is usually more than sufficient to let your Bichon know you disapprove of what he is doing. It is never necessary to strike a Bichon in any circumstance. A sharp *"No!"* is normally more than enough to get your point across.

Bichons make a great effort to please their owners and they are highly trainable as long as the trainer is not heavy handed. Training problems encountered are far more apt to be due to the owner than to a Bichon's lack of understanding or inability to learn.

Setting boundaries is as important to your Bichon's well-being as it is to your relationship with him. The sooner he understands there are rules that must be obeyed the easier it will be for him to become an enjoyable companion. The length of time it takes for you to establish and enforce those rules will determine how quickly this will come about. As previously mentioned, the Bichon is generally not particularly stubborn, but your guidance is needed so that he can understand the parameters within which he can operate.

Dealing with Aggression

Aggressive Bichon Frises are few and far between. On the very rare occasion that I have come across a Bichon that shows aggressive traits, an environment of abuse is far more apt to be the cause than heredity.

However, there is the rare Bichon inclined to fend off attacks by establishing his dominance and becoming aggressive. Manhandling and punishing a dog of this nature only serves to exacerbate the problem. The dog is in a self-protecting/aggressive mood and your attack only intensifies his mood.

Petting and trying to soothe your dog will not help the situation either. He may well take your soothing actions to mean approval for his behavior. You must put your dog under your authority by having him obey your command. This makes him submit to you. Responding to the *down* command puts him in a passive role rather than challenging or encouraging his unwanted behavior.

Boundaries, both behavioral and territorial, are very important for dogs to learn. Being taught early on what he can and cannot do leaves the dog with aggressive inclinations no opportunity to decide how to behave. It is up to the owner to establish the boundaries by which his or her companion will live.

Some dogs take their responsibility to protect too far and inadvertently create problem situations. They believe they have to defend their territory and, lacking guidance from their owners, establish their own boundaries. This must be nipped in the bud and redirected when it begins, and if it continues to be a problem, professional help must be obtained at once.

Helpful Hints

If you have ever watched nature films on television, you no doubt noticed that the pack leader eats first. If your problem dog eats his evening meal about the same time as you have your dinner, make it a point to eat first and then put his food dish down.

Those belly rubs your dog enjoys can serve a good purpose. The only way a dog can get a thoroughly good tummy rub is to lie on his back. This just happens to be a passive posture and a good one to get your dog accustomed to.

It is highly unlikely that you will ever have to deal with an aggressive Bichon Frise. Still, if a dog less than six months of age snaps and bites, it strongly indicates inherited bad temperament. Correcting or harnessing inherited bad temperament is a risky undertaking at best and usually leads to dire consequences at some point in the dog's life. Temperamentally untrustworthy puppies grow up to be temperamentally untrustworthy and dangerous adults.

Chapter Three

How to Choose a Bichon Frise

Learning as much as possible about the breed, making certain that the Bichon is the right dog for you, and finding a reputable breeder are the first steps to finding the healthy, well-socialized Bichon Frise for your household. Ask plenty of questions and choose wisely when you select your new companion. Bringing a Bichon into your household is a long-term commitment and you want to be certain the match is a good one.

Are You Ready for a Bichon Frise?

Every Bichon has his own personality, as does every potential Bichon owner. The breed also has distinct behavioral and inherited traits that are deeply ingrained. But how do you find the Bichon that will best suit you?

1. The Bichon is a versatile breed easily joining the more active members of the family in hikes and games and he is small and well-tempered enough to be a gentle companion to the less physically active members of the household. Do you know how you plan to spend time with your Bichon?
2. Are you looking for a dog that is versatile, devoted, and playful?
3. Coat care and upkeep is a big consideration with a Bichon. Are you willing to undertake this care yourself or pay for the services of a professional groomer?
4. Do you have the time to devote to exercising, raising, and training?
5. Can you afford to provide quality nutrition?
6. Do you have a veterinarian who can provide your Bichon Frise with regular and emergency health care?
7. Are you prepared to care for a dog for many years, possibly 15 or more?
8. Have you learned as much as possible about the Bichon breed, compared it to other breeds, and still believe the Bichon is the best match for you?

COMPATIBILITY Is a Bichon Frise the Best Breed for You?

ENERGY LEVEL	• • • •
PERSONAL ATTENTION REQUIREMENT	• • • •
EXERCISE REQUIREMENT	• •
PLAYFULNESS	• • • •
AFFECTION LEVEL	• • • • •
FRIENDLINESS TOWARD OTHER PETS	• • • •
FRIENDLINESS TOWARD STRANGERS	• • •
FRIENDLINESS TOWARD CHILDREN	• • • •
EASE OF TRAINING	• • •
EASE OF HOUSE TRAINING	• •
GROOMING REQUIREMENTS	• • • • •
SPACE REQUIREMENTS	• • •
OK FOR BEGINNERS	• • • •

5 Dots = Highest rating on scale

If you've answered yes to these questions, you may just be ready to join the ranks of those who love, own, and appreciate the many talents and traits of the Bichon Frise.

Finding a Breeder

Of all the questions that must be given serious consideration, none is as critical as where your puppy or adult Bichon will come from. Bichons are advertised in the newspaper, appear in pet shops, are from a litter bred by someone down the block, and are on countless web sites. All sources claim to have just the dog that you are looking for, but in this case, haste more often than not makes waste.

Because of my longtime association with the breed I regularly get calls from individuals who are looking to purchase a Bichon. Since I am no longer actively breeding Bichons, I try to have a list handy of breeders I know and respect who currently have puppies available.

Most legitimate breeders breed only occasionally and there are times when I know that there are no puppies currently available in the vicinity of the person who is making the inquiry. My advice then to the prospective purchaser is to give me a bit of time to locate a good breeder who might help them in their search. All too often, by the time I find the right source

BE PREPARED! A Dozen Questions the Breeder Will Ask You

1. Why do you want a Bichon Frise?
2. Do you have experience with Bichons, or have you owned a Bichon in the past?
3. Are you prepared to have your pet quality Bichon spayed or neutered?
4. Do you have children and, if so, how old are they?
5. Do you have other pets? What type are they?
6. Do you enjoy grooming and do you have time and patience to learn how to do it right? Can you afford to hire a groomer on a frequent, regular basis?
7. Do you have a fenced-in yard, patio, or safe enclosure for a Bichon Frise?
8. How many hours a day are you home? Do you have time to care for your Bichon Frise, including playtime and daily walks?
9. Can you provide the name and phone number of your veterinarian for a reference and follow-up contact?
10. Can the breeder meet all members of your family who will be living with the Bichon Frise?
11. Do you plan to take your Bichon Frise with you on trips and vacations? If not, who will care for your Bichon Frise while you are away?
12. Do you promise to contact the breeder immediately in the event that you are no longer able to keep or care for your Bichon Frise?

BE PREPARED! Ten Questions to Ask the Breeder

1. How old are the pups and what colors, sexes, and ages are available?
2. Are the pups registered with a recognized kennel club, such as the American Kennel Club?
3. Have the pups been examined and vaccinated by a veterinarian? If so, which vaccinations have the pups received? Do the pups have any special health certifications from veterinary specialists?
4. How many pups are in the litter and at what age were they weaned?
5. Have the pups been treated or tested for internal and external parasites?
6. Does the breeder keep track of and test for health problems? Are there any known health problems in the puppy's family lines?
7. Have the pups received any basic training, including housetraining, crate training, or leash training?
8. What kind of food do the pups eat? How much and how often do they eat?
9. Can I see the parents and littermates of the pup and the environment where the puppies are raised?
10. Will the breeder take the dog back if at some time you are unable to care for him?

the person who called has found "just the right puppy" at a pet shop or from someone down the street whose lovely little "Trixie" has just had a litter sired by a dog her owner met at the local dog park. As time passes I begin to get distress signals from the buyer, wondering if it is normal for the breed to have so many health problems or if I can recommend a veterinarian who is not quite as expensive as the one they are using, because health costs are soaring.

Make sure that the Bichon you purchase comes from a legitimate and respected breeder. There are other methods that may prove satisfactory, but none as reliable as seeking the help of someone who has had longtime experience with the Bichon Frise breed and has stock that is being carefully supervised and tested for health and temperament.

- Good breeders support the breed in many ways—they belong to Bichon Frise or all-breed clubs. They show their dogs or participate in some of the numerous activities such as Obedience or Agility Trials.
- Good breeders are happy to let you see the environment where the puppies are born and raised.
- Good breeders are knowledgeable about their dogs and they are ready and willing to discuss any problems that exist in their, or the breed's, pedigrees.

- Good breeders interview you to determine whether you'll be a good Bichon owner. They want to be as sure that their puppies are getting into the right hands as you are that you are getting a sound and healthy companion.
- Good breeders provide puppies with their inoculations and guarantees and encourage you to continue on with the meticulous health care they have given every puppy they breed.

Buyer Beware

Hidden recessives in pedigrees can produce health and temperament problems that make dog ownership an incredibly expensive and complicated experience—to say nothing of the toll they can take on your emotions. The Bichon Frise has become popular enough to attract the attention of the commercially minded and the breed has appeared in puppy mills across the country where puppies are mass produced and cared for by those who are far more concerned with the amount of profit a puppy will bring in than what a good Bichon puppy is or the care it needs.

This is not to say that everyone who attempts to sell you a puppy does so unscrupulously. A one-dog owner who breeds his or her female to the dog down the street, as purebred and registered as both parents might be, may have no idea as to the genetic problems the pair might carry and how they will manifest in the offspring.

This also applies to classified ads in the newspapers and puppies you may see staring out the window of a mall pet shop. The unknowns may be even greater. So before deciding to purchase from either source, do your research. Investigate the reputation of the source, try to talk to previous buyers, or even search for reviews on the Internet. Also, all puppies should be up-to-date with their exams and immunizations, so make sure to ask for a copy of the puppy's medical records. You can never be too careful when making the final purchase of your new puppy.

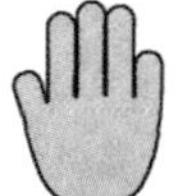

CAUTION

Healthy, well-bred Bichons also end their lives in the nation's animal shelters for various reasons. This is why a responsible breeder will insist that they be given first opportunity to rehome any dog they sell if the buyer is unable to keep the dog. Still, there are many Bichons to be found in city and county maintained shelters. If you are considering adopting from a shelter, investigate the background of the dog and find out just why he wound up in the shelter in the first place.

Pet Stores

Who can resist that winsome puppy peering at us from behind the pet shop window glass? Even songs have been written about obtaining a puppy from a pet shop. Those of you who are old enough will remember Patti Page wistfully singing "(How Much Is) That Doggie in the Window" back in the early 1950s. It is probably one of the simplest tunes ever written with lyrics a child

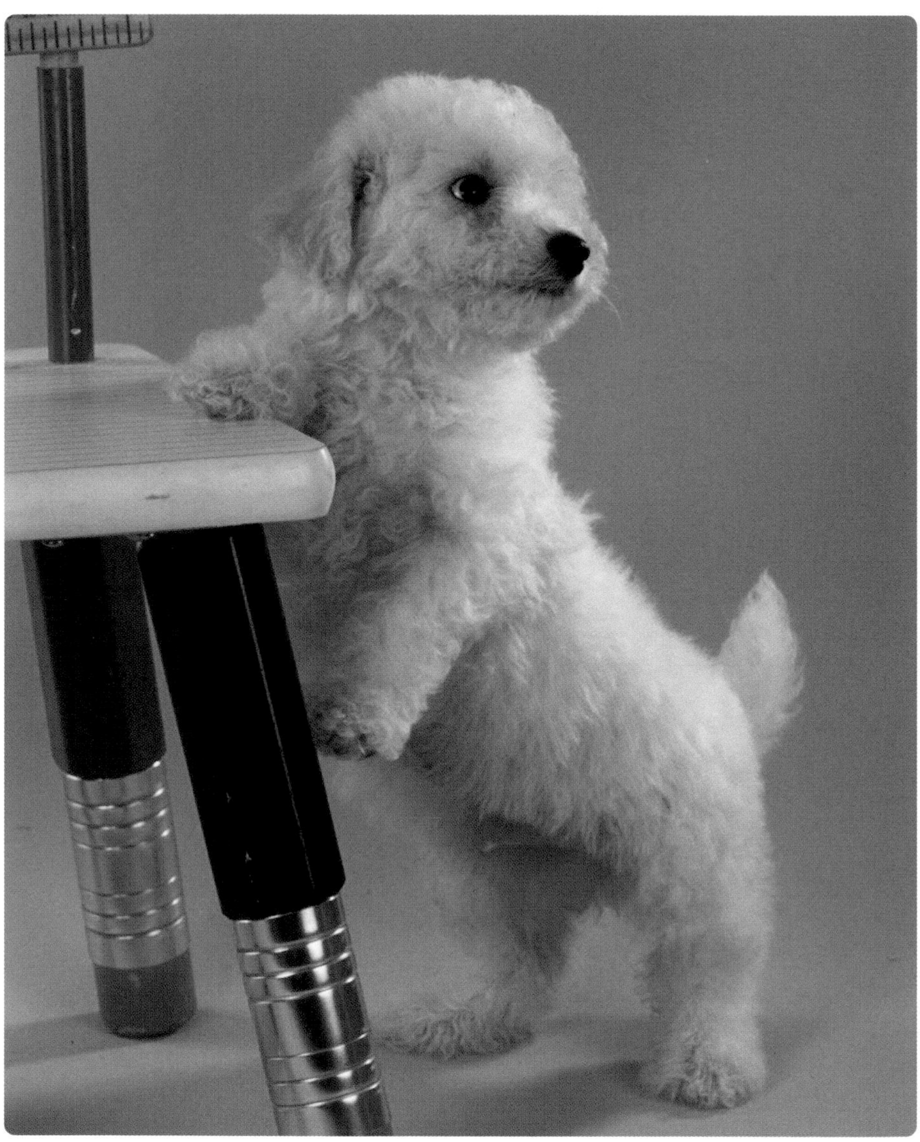

could write, but it has become a "golden hit," a top seller, and a standard on more albums than you can possibly imagine.

Why does that song have such an enduring quality? Probably because every single person that has ever passed by a pet shop window has had his heartstrings tugged by that tail-wagging, soulful-eyed puppy begging to be taken home. Pet shops provide instant gratification that has defined the meaning of the term: I want a puppy, I want it now, I go to the mall pet shop, I get a puppy, I pay my money, I come home with a puppy. It's as simple and quick as all that.

Just how *fortunate* a transaction that is remains to be seen. Average pet shop owners might not always have knowledge of the background of the puppies offered for sale in their shops. Although there are exceptions, generally speaking the puppies come to the shops from outside sources that provide minimal history regarding parents of the puppies or the manner in which they were raised.

Pet shop prices can sometimes be higher than those charged by experienced and reliable breeders, but guarantees are fewer. To compound the risk, pet shops often hire clerks to handle the sale of their animals. Lack of knowledge on the part of these individuals may often have them making claims that are unsubstantiated. It is indeed a situation in which you must be sure to research before you buy.

Newspaper and Internet Ads

Puppies offered for sale in newspaper ads or in general web site ads are sometimes those that are the result of someone deciding to breed their "purebred and registered" female and having chosen the "purebred and registered" dog down the block as the sire. If the puppies are raised by concerned individuals who have taken the time to educate themselves on proper care and nutrition, your chances of getting a physically and mentally sound puppy are good. However, even the most concerned novice in the world cannot know what genetic problems have been created by the introduction of the two parents responsible for the birth.

Hobby Breeders

Hobby breeders are usually those individuals who are members of their breed's parent club (in this case the BFCA) and who abide by the code of ethics established by their organization. They breed dogs in a small way, perhaps only one litter every year or so, but the dogs they do breed are from a program that is genetically well thought out. Their dogs have also been accomplished in the various competitions for their breed: conformation, obedience, agility, and so on.

There is much thought that goes into each and every breeding these breeders make. Probably the biggest difference between the Hobby Breeder and a large, professional kennel specializing in a breed is numbers. The Hobby Breeder is severely restricted in the number of dogs he or she can keep and in the number of litters they are able to accommodate.

Bichon Rescue

There are other very satisfactory methods by which a happy, healthy, and well-bred Bichon can be obtained, particularly if the buyer is not dead set on buying a very young puppy. Nicely bred Bichons are often available through the many Bichon rescue agencies throughout the country. Many of these organizations can trace the background of the dogs in their care and observe

BE PREPARED! **Adopting a Rescue Dog**

Before adopting a resue shelter dog, determine the following:

1. The age and sexual status (puppy or sexually mature).
2. Whether or not the dog has been neutered or spayed.
3. Attitude toward children, other dogs, other animals in prior home.
4. Extent of former training.
5. Cleanliness level (housebroken to outdoors/indoors).
6. On-leash behavior.
7. Level of food and/or toy guarding and aggressiveness.

their health, character, and temperament. There are many reasons why owners give up Bichons of various ages. What was once a perfect home for a Bichon can be disrupted by divorce, illness, or a move that makes it impossible to keep a dog. A career change may significantly reduce the amount of time available for responsible dog care. Many rescue Bichons are housebroken and well trained; others may have behavior problems, especially if they were continuously left home alone.

Rescuing a Bichon can be very rewarding. The Bichon Frise Club of America (BFCA) is comprised of dedicated breeders and exhibitors who work together to make sure that every Bichon that needs rehoming is placed in the correct hands. The organization will be able to put you in touch with the rescue chapter groups that exist in your area.

This information may be readily available at the shelter or it may take a bit of sleuthing on your part. Regardless of how much time and effort that might take, it is time well spent for obvious reasons—you are looking for a mentally and physically sound friend and companion who will live with you for many years to come.

Choosing a Bichon Frise Puppy

There are some things that you can pretty well rely on in obtaining your Bichon in so long as you are in the hands of a respected breeder. Your Bichon will have all the basic breed characteristics: he will have a white curly coat, at mature age he will be somewhere under 12 inches measured from the top of the shoulder to the ground, he will have a dark nose and dark eyes, and he will have an amiable attitude toward people and other animals.

If you are in the right hands you will be able to feel confident that the puppy you are looking at was raised with health considerations foremost in mind. He will be vigorous and sound, bright-eyed, and pleasingly plump but not fat.

CHECKLIST

Is the Puppy Healthy?

- ✔ **Coat:** Should be clean, soft, and white. Skin eruptions are warning signs that the puppy may be sick. Flaky or sparse coats can indicate both internal and external parasites.
- ✔ **Conformation:** Avoid any puppy that seems bony, undernourished, or bloated.
- ✔ **Ears:** The inside of the ears should be pink and clean. There should be no discharge or strong odor.
- ✔ **Eyes:** The puppy's eyes should be clear, bright, and dark in color.
- ✔ **Mouth:** Gums should be firm and pink with clean white teeth. The under jaw should not be crooked. The teeth should meet in what is called a scissors bite (the upper front teeth slightly overlapping the bottom front teeth). Discuss any questions about the alignment of the puppy's teeth or jaw with the breeder.
- ✔ **Nose:** A crusted or running nose is a danger signal.

That said, there are always individual differences within any litter of puppies of any breed. Quiet, boisterous, or needy, a myriad of traits make up the individual personality of every puppy born. The experienced breeder takes account of these differences and makes every effort to make sure that the right puppy goes home with the correct owner. Your wants and needs also help determine where to start the hunt for your ideal Bichon.

The Bichon from Cradle to Adulthood

The average person would be amazed at the amount of time experienced breeders of quality Bichons spend observing their puppies, even while the puppies are still in the whelping box nursing on their mother. They mentally evaluate each and every puppy in the litter during the early weeks, even before eyes are open, and record the characteristics they observe for each puppy. The puppies benefit in that they become accustomed to being handled by humans, even before they have a clue as to what a human is. When the puppies do open their eyes, they are already comfortable with the touch and scent of humans. Sight then identifies where these pleasurable sensations are coming from.

Two–Three Weeks

The buyer is seldom given the opportunity to become involved with a litter of less than eight-week old puppies, since breeders do their utmost to avoid the possibility of strangers bringing communicable canine diseases into the

puppy nursery. However, this does not mean that the puppies are devoid of human contact or that there is nothing going on in the development of the newborn puppies.

During this time a puppy's eyes will open, and he'll slowly start to respond to light and movement and sounds around him. He'll become more mobile during this period and make clumsy attempts to get his legs under him. He will start to recognize his dam and his littermates by sight rather than by scent or their ability to give off sustenance or warmth. Toys and strange objects will even draw his attention at this point.

Three–Four Weeks

During the three–four weeks period, a Bichon puppy undergoes rapid sensory development. He becomes fully aware of his environment and begins to recognize his human caretakers. It's best to avoid loud noises or sudden changes when possible during this period—negative events can have a serious impact on his personality and development at this vulnerable stage. Puppies learn how to be a dog during this time, so it's essential that they stay with Mom and littermates.

The character and stability of the puppies' dam is extremely important to the Bichon puppy at this age. As much as the breeder wants to avoid loud noises and unplanned-for situations, they do occur. Objects fall crashing to the ground, the doorbell or phone rings, someone slams a door. These are unavoidable situations and a part of real life.

An unstable dam can overreact to these unexpected situations and panic. Rest assured, her puppies sense this panic and react accordingly. A stable mother takes all these things in stride and puppies noting her calm demeanor learn to accept these unusual situations as part of day-to-day living.

Four–Seven Weeks

The four–seven week period of a Bichon puppy's life is a critical one. He's learning how to get along with his littermates. He also begins to learn his place in the "pack." The dominant pups will begin to flex their little muscles and the more passive members of the litter will learn how to cope with the family bullies.

The puppies' mom will begin the weaning process about this time. With this comes her initial lessons in puppy "manners," which include having the pups understand that she is the leader of the pack. As weaning begins, the pups are introduced to food other than mother's milk.

Breeders continue handling the pups frequently and briefly each day. Puppies removed from the nest too early can become extremely nervous, prone to barking, and have a more difficult time with socialization and training. Most Bichon breeders leave their puppies with their mom and siblings until they are at least eight weeks of age, often longer, for optimum social development.

The Bichon breeders I have known believe that the three–sixteen week period is the time period during which "puppies learn to be dogs." That is, they learn all the little social skills necessary to ensure that they grow up to be well-adjusted canines.

Eight Weeks–Three Months

At this time, the Bichon puppy's bladder and bowels are beginning to come under some control and it is the time when he becomes capable of sleeping through the night. It is usually at about three months that breeders allow their puppies to go to their new homes. It is also the time that the Bichon puppy is capable of learning simple commands, like: *come, sit, stay, down,* etc. Leash training can begin at this time as well.

It is critical to remember that a puppy that is taken away from its littermates at this time should never be placed in an isolated situation away from human contact. (This is not a good time to bring home a puppy to a situation in which humans are away all day long.) Human contact must replace what he enjoyed with his littermates and mother.

Some Bichon puppies denied constant human contact at this stage become terrified of any, even remotely strange, situation or person. Not all dogs experience this, but many do, and they'll appear terrified over things that they took in stride before. This is not a good time to engage in loud reprimands or to allow traumatic events to take place.

Three–Six Months

By this time, most Bichon puppies have become adjusted to their new homes, completely forgotten about their Moms and littermates, and the new owner has become the important figure in their lives. They are also becoming a little more independent. It is not unusual for the quick-to-learn puppy to start ignoring the same commands that only the day before he responded to with glee. This stage is comparable to the human toddler's "terrible two's." Human parents need no further explanation of this stage, but Bichon owners who have never raised a child have to understand that their little whiz-bang canine is learning how to establish himself as an individual. Firm but gentle reinforcement of commands and training is what is required here.

Pierre's urge to please may decline significantly at this time and since he will be going through a teething cycle, he will also be looking for things to chew on to relieve the pain and pressure.

Six–Eighteen Months

Young adulthood at last! Pierre is young, he's exuberant, and he's learning all the things he needs to become a full-fledged adult dog, but don't sit back and relax entirely yet. Be realistic in your expectations: Pierre may look like an adult, but he isn't as seasoned and experienced as you might expect. You can start more advanced training at this point and try to include more people and animals in his life. Allow him to interact with nonthreatening or nonaggressive dogs.

Puppy or Adult?

Bichons have different needs at different stages of their lives. Those needs and your lifestyle must correlate. Prior to immunization, puppies are very susceptible to infectious diseases. Many such diseases may be transmitted on the clothing and hands of people. Also consider how much time you have to devote to a very young puppy. Will someone be available to take the puppy outdoors every few hours to assist the house training process? If not, a young adult, a mature dog, or perhaps even an old-timer might be a much better choice.

Male or Female?

The Bichon Frise is a breed in which sex makes little difference. The male Bichon is just as loving, devoted, and trainable as his female counterpart. There are some sex-related differences to consider, however. A male dog of any breed has a natural instinct to lift his leg and "mark" his territory. He has an innate urge to establish the fact that everything in and around his home belongs to him. This unfortunately may include your designer drapes or the stately evergreens gracing your garden.

Females have their own set of problems. Females have their semi-annual heat cycles that commence anywhere from around nine months to a year of age. During these cycles of approximately 21 days, she must to be confined to avoid soiling her surroundings with the bloody discharge that accompanies estrus and to prevent males from gaining access to her and getting her pregnant.

Having your pet Bichon altered can eliminate both these male and female problems. Spaying and neutering save the pet owner all the headaches of sexually related problems without changing the basic character or attitude of their dogs.

Show Dog or Companion?

The older a Bichon is at time of selection the more apt you are to know how good a dog he or she will be at maturity. If dog shows or breeding are in the future for your Bichon this is very important. The most any breeder can say about an eight-week-old Bichon puppy is that he has or does not have "show potential." Anyone seriously interested in showing or breeding Bichons should look for a puppy that is somewhere around the age of five or six months. At this age things like dentition, soundness, and attitude, along with many other important characteristics, can more accurately be determined.

If breeding or owning winning show dogs is your intention, you absolutely must seek the assistance of an experienced breeder who has a record of having produced outstanding dogs through the years. An experienced breeder, using the same bloodlines over an extended period of time, knows what clues to look for in selecting youngsters with show potential.

Price

It is difficult, if not impossible, to suggest the price of a Bichon Frise. Much depends on the kind of puppy you are looking for. Companion, breeding prospect, or show prospects command different prices. Prices can also vary considerably by the area of the country in which the dog is purchased.

Reputable breeders invest considerable time, skill, and effort to make sure they have the best possible breeding stock. This costs a great deal of money and the price structure of their puppies will be higher than that of someone who has not incurred the expense of the veterinary supervision and testing needed to keep their dogs as free from hereditary defects as possible. A puppy purchased from an established and successful breeder may cost a bit more initially, but the small additional investment brings you a great deal more for what you spend.

Temperament

Regardless of the age or purpose of your Bichon or the place that he comes from, there is nothing more important than temperament in the Bichon that joins your household. Canine behaviorists have devised tests to indicate the nature and possible adult temperament of puppies. Simple tests can give general indications of the level of independence, confidence, and sociability a puppy has achieved. The puppy's reaction to these tests can also give the owner clues to the best way to approach early training.

Paperwork

Before you leave with your Bichon tucked under your arm, there are some very important transactions that have to take place. First off, the seller will want to get paid. Cash is always appreciated, as is a cashier's check. If your payment is a personal check, the seller may wish to have you come back to pick up your puppy when the check has cleared the bank.

On the day the actual sale is completed you are entitled to four very important documents:

1. Health record: Details of all home and veterinary care along with an inoculation schedule.
2. Pedigree: A chronological list of the puppy's ancestors.
3. Registration Certificate: The canine world's birth certificate.
4. Sales contract: A written agreement that lists everything that both the buyer and seller agree to be responsible for.

CAUTION

The chances that your dog will be infected with rabies by another companion dog are highly remote. However, this doesn't preclude the possibility of your Bichon coming in contact with wild animals that have contracted the disease. Do not overlook the importance of inoculating against this possibility.

There should be no extra charge for these documents. Good breeders supply them with every puppy they sell.

Health record Your puppy's health record should indicate what kind of veterinary treatment the puppy has been given since birth. This will include a record of exams along with dates and type of medication used for each worming.

The record must contain an inoculation schedule. Most Bichon Frise breeders have begun the necessary inoculation series for their puppies by the time they are seven to eight weeks of age. These inoculations protect the puppies against hepatitis, leptospirosis, distemper, and canine parvovirus. These are all deadly communicable diseases that will be dealt with at greater length in Chapter 6. It is important to understand that these are diseases that can kill your puppy seemingly overnight and even if the puppy escapes death, it will invariably be permanently impaired.

A rabies inoculation is also necessary and is a requirement in obtaining a license to own a dog but in most cases it is not administered until a puppy

ACTIVITIES Temperament Tests

Test #1 Sociability

Clap your hands and call to the puppy.

1. Does the puppy look up and at you?
2. Does he approach readily?
3. Does he do so in a friendly, enthusiastic manner?

Positive response is a good sign of sociability. Disinterest on the part of the puppy can indicate a lack of early human interaction.

Test #2 Confidence

Make eye contact with the puppy.

1. Does the puppy return the eye contact?

This is usually a good indication of confidence on the puppy's part. A puppy that does not return eye contact can indicate problems—either in temperament or vision.

Test #3 Independence

Call to the puppy when he is interested elsewhere.

1. As soon as your call gets the puppy's attention, begin to walk away.
2. Does he quickly attempt to follow you?
3. As you increase the speed at which you are walking does the puppy make an effort to keep up?

The more dependent puppy will make every effort to stay near you. The attention of the more gregarious and independent puppy will be distracted easily and he will perhaps wander off on his own.

is four to six months of age or older. Local ordinances have a bearing on this and the rabies shot may be necessary before that time. Check with your veterinarian, who will know what situations exist that are peculiar to your area.

Immunization schedules are changing and the pet may not need annual boosters unless required by local law (as with rabies) and titers can be checked after the first combination booster to determine the need for future boosters. If the dog needs both the rabies shot and the combination shot, the BFCA strongly recommends that these shots be separated by at least a month in order not to stress the immune system of your Bichon.

A puppy should never be taken away from its original home before these initial inoculations have been at least started. There is a prescribed series of inoculations developed to combat these infectious diseases and it is extremely important that you obtain a record of their number and the kind your puppy has been given. You must also have the dates the shots were administered and the type and make of serum used. In this way the

FYI: Pedigree Defined

All purebred dogs have a pedigree, but this does not imply that a dog is of show quality. Some unscrupulous dog sellers attempting to get a higher price out of an unsuspecting buyer insist that a pedigree has some special significance—that it indicates show or championship potential in some way. This is not true. A pedigree simply lists the dog's ancestors and authenticates that all of the dogs listed are indeed purebred Bichons. Every dog in the pedigree may have been nothing more than pet quality. Beware of such tactics.

veterinarian you choose will be able to continue with the appropriate inoculations as needed.

Pedigree The pedigree is your dog's family tree. The breeder and/or seller of every AKC registered dog should supply the buyer with a copy of this document. The pedigree lists your puppy's ancestors back to at least the third generation by giving each of the registered names.

A pedigree is read from left to right. The first two names in the first column on the left are the puppy's sire and dam. The sire's ancestry, reading left to right, occupies the top half of the pedigree. The dam's ancestors appear on the bottom half.

In most cases pedigrees are handwritten or typed by the breeder. These unofficial documents give you your puppy's ancestry, but like any document prepared by a human, they can contain spelling errors and other assorted mistakes. If you wish to obtain an official pedigree, only the country's official registration source (in the United States, the AKC or UKC) can issue them.

Pedigrees may also list the titles the individual dogs in the pedigree have earned. The titles and their appropriate abbreviations are earned for excellence of conformation through to basic and advanced obedience accomplishments.

Kennel club registration As with the official pedigree, a registration certificate is issued by a country's governing kennel club. When you transfer the ownership of your Bichon from the breeder's name to your own, the transaction is entered on this certificate. Once mailed to the AKC, it is permanently recorded in their computerized files. Most breeders like to insert an official name for the puppy on the registration using their kennel name as a prefix. The reason for doing this is that it permanently associates that puppy with the breeder. Actually, it is a compliment to the puppy to have the breeder think enough of him to insure the association. You, of course, can call the puppy anything you choose.

When you purchase a puppy the individual registration or "blue slip" is transferred to you. The slip must be completed and returned to the AKC with necessary fee no later than 12 months from the date of the puppy's birth. The puppy's birth date is printed on the blue slip itself.

Sales contract A reputable breeder will supply a written agreement that lists everything that he or she is responsible for in connection with the sale of the Bichon described. The contract will also list all the things the buyer is responsible for before the sale is actually final. The contract should be dated and signed by both the seller and the buyer. Sales contracts vary but all assurances and anything that is an exception to the outright and final sale should be itemized. Some of these conditions should be

1. Sale is contingent upon dog passing a veterinarian's examination within 24–48 hours after it leaves the seller's premises. Clear statement of refund policy.
2. Any conditions prevail regarding the seller's requirement for neutering of the dog sold.
3. Indication that a limited registration accompanies dog (that is, the dog is ineligible to have offspring registered by the AKC).
4. Arrangements that must be followed in the event the buyer is unable to keep the dog regardless of length of time that elapses after sale.
5. Conditions that exist should dog develop genetic bone or eye diseases at maturity.

The contents of sales contracts vary considerably, but the buyer should read the contract carefully to make sure he or she understands what is included and for what both the buyer and seller are responsible.

Diet Sheet

Your Bichon is the happy, healthy youngster he is because the breeder has properly fed and cared for him every step of the way. All established breeders have their own experienced way of doing so. Because they have been successful in breeding and raising their puppies, most breeders give the new owner a written record that details the amount and kind of food a puppy has been receiving. They will normally give you enough of the food the puppy has been eating to last until you are able to go out and purchase the necessary products yourself. Do follow these recommendations to the letter at least for the first month or two after the puppy comes to live with you.

The diet sheet should indicate the number of times a day your puppy has been accustomed to being fed. Following the prescribed procedure will reduce the chance of upset stomach and loose stools.

Usually a breeder's diet sheet projects the increases and changes in food that will be necessary as your puppy grows from week to week. If the sheet does not include this information, ask the breeder for suggestions regarding increases and the eventual changeover to adult food.

CAUTION

Some breeders add vitamin supplements to their dogs' and puppies' diets as a matter of course. Other breeders are adamantly opposed to supplements when well-balanced and nutritious food is given. Be sure to clearly understand what your breeder's thoughts are on this issue and act accordingly.

Chapter Four

Caring for a Bichon Frise Puppy

Your Bichon's age as he first enters your household determines how you will handle his arrival and what you'll have to deal with in the following weeks and months. For many people a very young puppy will not work due to the constant care and presence he requires. Therefore a puppy of five or six months of age might well be a better choice.

Breed Development

Like all living things, Bichons have different needs at different stages of their lives. They will react to their new environment accordingly and you should be prepared for this.

Eight–Twelve Weeks

During these first few weeks of life, there is nothing a Bichon puppy has greater need for than his mother and littermates. They provide sustenance, comfort, and warmth. During this period the pups find out other creatures do exist and they have to be coped with. At first, life is nothing more than mother and the nourishment she provides, but shortly the puppy finds he must compete for what he needs. Bichon moms also teach their offspring a great deal during these first weeks of life. It is extremely important to a puppy's development that he has this time with mother and littermates.

As little Pierre approaches his eighth week, it is the perfect time to introduce him to the world outside his nesting box and give him some time alone with humans. At this age he is mature enough to readjust to some strange sights and sounds easily, but not old enough to have developed strong attachments. Puppies that remain too long as part of a litter without an opportunity to experience a bit of life on their own can identify solely with their siblings rather than transferring this relationship to humans.

Most Bichon breeders like to keep their puppies until they are sure of their health and temperament and seldom release them before 12 weeks. However, most canine behaviorists believe that eight weeks of age is the optimal time for a puppy to go to his new home. This will depend entirely upon the wishes of the person from whom you obtain your Bichon.

Twelve–Sixteen Weeks

At this age everything in life is an experiment for the Bichon puppy. Curiosity is endless, and he is ready to take on new events and quick to develop a sense of belonging. This is the time electrical wires must be pulled, fences must be climbed, and all objects tested to determine their chewability. At the same time your Bichon puppy is pretty much dependent on you and wants to be with you wherever you go. This is the proper time for him to learn the good puppy basics. Commands like *"No," "Come," "Sit,"* and *"Stay,"* should be part of his daily lessons. Training sessions shouldn't be long, but they should be regular. Confidence begins building at this stage and the early dependency that was so typical may be diminishing almost overnight.

Breed Needs

Discuss your home situation with your breeder and explain what you will and won't be able to do for the new puppy. With this information the breeder can decide the best age for you to take your puppy home.

Sixteen–Twenty-four Weeks

This is the age that takes the most patience. Think of Pierre as a human teenager and you will fully understand what is going on. Defiance, independence, can't remember that command are all perfectly normal and completely aggravating.

Keeping up training lessons is critical through this stage. Your puppy is testing you and just searching for those little chinks in your control that he can slip through. Your puppy is attempting to be the brave little soul you encouraged him to be; the problem is he doesn't know exactly how to do that. It is up to you to guide him through to the other end of the tunnel.

The Basics

It is important for both the new puppy's well-being and your nerves that every effort be made to make his transition from kennel to home as painless as possible. Before you set off for the nearest pet emporium, make a list of all the basics you'll need. Without a list you could easily be overwhelmed with the incredible number of choices and gadgets these pet supermarkets now carry. Having everything in place before little Pierre arrives will save you a good many costly days and sleepless nights.

You are going to need equipment to keep that little tyke busy, other equipment to keep him in, and still other equipment to keep him out. There has to be a place for him to play and a place to sleep. You'll need some toys for training and some toys just for fun. Unfortunately, the one thing you won't be able to find in any shop is patience—and that's the thing you'll need most. You will have to supply it yourself and believe me, there will be times when you will have need for far more than you ever imagined possible.

If this is your first dog, you will probably need to start from scratch. If you've had a dog before, check to make sure that what you have will adapt to the size and needs of your Bichon puppy.

The Must-Have Shopping List

Before bringing your new puppy home, it's important to have some essential items to ensure his happiness and safety.

Paneled fence partition or pen to cordon off a living area for the puppy Exercise pens about three feet high are available at most pet shops. The kitchen is an ideal place to set up this area as there is usually some member of the family in the room throughout the day to keep the puppy company, and kitchen flooring is usually easiest to clean up.

SHOPPING LIST

Must Haves

- ✔ Fence partition or pen
- ✔ Crates and cages
- ✔ Feeding bowls and water dishes
- ✔ Food
- ✔ Brushes, combs, and nail clippers
- ✔ Collars and leashes
- ✔ Toys
- ✔ Odor neutralizers and cleaners
- ✔ Chewing deterrents

This fenced off area provides an area of safety for the puppy, keeping him out of mischief and protecting him from older or larger dogs in the household who may not be entirely pleased with the new addition. It also gives the family cat the option of checking out the new intruder without being harassed in the process.

Most Bichon puppies love children but it may take a bit of time for the unaccustomed puppy to feel comfortable around them. The fencing keeps the child at a safe distance and gives the puppy an opportunity to accept them gradually.

Crates and cages Fiberglass airline-type crates are ideal for Bichons. A medium-sized crate, approximately 20 inches (51 cm) high by 24 inches (61 cm) wide by 30 inches (77 cm) long can be partitioned to accommodate a young puppy and is just right for the fully-grown Bichon. Check to see if the manufacturer's warranty states the crate is "airline approved"—just in case you and Pierre decide to vacation together. When traveling by air this approval is a requirement.

In warm climates, some Bichon owners prefer the metal wire-type crates in the home and car as they provide better air circulation. The wire crates come in all sizes as well and some have the additional advantage of being collapsible so that they can be folded flat if you need to transport them.

Feeding bowls and water dishes These are available in many different materials. Choose something that is non-breakable and not easy to tip over. Many are constructed with wide bases that are less likely to be overturned. A rambunctious puppy will very quickly learn to upset the water bowl and relish turning his entire living area into a swimming pool. Stainless steel bowls are recommended because they eliminate the worry of the toxic content of some plastics, and dogs and puppies are not beyond chewing (and trying to digest!) plastic bowls.

Food The breeder from whom you purchased your puppy knows what works best and can recommend the best food for your Bichon.

Brushes, combs, and nail clippers Your pet shop can help you pick out the type of grooming equipment you will need for your new puppy. As your Bichon matures you will need more sophisticated equipment to keep him looking as he should (a list of that equipment is included in Chapter 8).

Collars and leashes Just as there are many brands of food, there are also varieties of different leashes and collars to choose from. For puppy training and leash breaking, there are soft fabric collars available that weigh next to nothing and will be accepted by your puppy quickly and easily. To begin, a very soft length of clothesline will suffice as a leash.

Toys Puppies need several toys of different kinds to keep them occupied, exercised, and out of mischief. However, don't give your dog so many toys that the dog begins to think everything that exists is a toy of some kind.

The toys you choose can be anything that is appropriate for the age of your Bichon. Just be sure the toys are safe—without buttons or strings that can be chewed off or swallowed. Also avoid balls made of soft material that can be chewed apart and avoid hard plastic toys that can splinter easily.

HOME BASICS

That's Not a Toy!

Never give your puppy old and discarded shoes or stockings to play with. A puppy is unable to determine the difference between "old" and "new." As far as he is concerned, your old slipper smells and tastes exactly like the pair of Manolo Blahniks you may have only worn a few times.

Teddy bears also don't make good dog toys. Most have plastic or glass buttons for eyes that can be swallowed, ears that can be torn off and swallowed, and stuffing that can be ripped out and ingested. You and your dog may have to spend some very unpleasant and costly time at the veterinarian's office when this happens.

Make sure any toys you give your puppy or even grown dog are too large for them to become lodged in the mouth or caught in the throat. Large knucklebones are not technically toys, but your dog will undoubtedly think otherwise. A dog can spend the best part of an afternoon gnawing away on the same bone!

Kong toys are wonderful as are most of the heavy rope toys. The Kong toy is especially good because it is made of nearly indestructible rubber and has a hole in the bottom so that a little dab of peanut butter or some other treat can be stuffed into it. This will keep the dog occupied for hours on end.

Household odor neutralizers and cleaners There are few things that are more unpleasant (especially to non-dog owners) than a household that reeks of doggy odor. Pet shops and supermarkets carry all kinds of odor neutralizers and cleaners that can ensure an odor free home.

Chewing deterrents There is a product called Bitter Apple that most dogs (but not all) find unpleasant in taste. It will help keep your puppy from chewing anything it is applied to. This non-toxic cream can be used to coat everything from electrical wires to chair legs.

Housetraining

Some Bichons can prove to be a real challenge when it comes to housebreaking. It seems that males can learn this lesson a bit easier than their sisters. Persistence counts here and negligence on your part even for a day or two can set your puppy back weeks.

Helpful Hints

It is far more difficult to achieve housebreaking success when you have to correct a behavior that has established itself rather than simply teach a puppy the correct way to do it in the first place. Once a puppy has become accustomed to relieving himself at will, you will have to undo that behavior before beginning the correct process.

The Crate Method

The method that I have found works best with both puppies and young adults is the cage or crate method, which is based on the notion that dogs do not like to eliminate near where they eat and sleep.

I've had first-time dog owners see the crate method of housebreaking as cruel initially, but those same people have always returned later to thank me for having suggested using this method in the first place.

Most dogs think of their crate as their "den." All dogs need a place of their own to retreat to and you will probably find that your dog will consider his cage or crate that place. The cage or crate used for housebreaking should be large enough for the dog to stand up, lie down, and stretch out comfortably, but no larger.

Begin to feed your Bichon puppy in his crate. Keep the door closed and latched while he is eating. When the meal is finished, open the cage and carry him outdoors to the spot where you want him to eliminate. It is important to go back to the same spot each and every time. Doing so will reinforce that this is the place for doing his business and will save you hours of cleanup time when droppings need only be collected from one location rather than from all over the yard.

If you are not able to watch your dog every minute, he should be in his cage or crate with the door securely latched. Each time you put your dog inside the crate, give him a small treat. Throw the treat to the back of the crate and encourage him to walk in on his own. When he does, give him lots of praise and perhaps another piece of the treat through the wires of the cage.

Do not succumb to your Bichon's initial complaints about being in his crate. The puppy must learn to stay in his cage and to do so without complaining. If you respond to his vocal demands to be let out, you are sure to

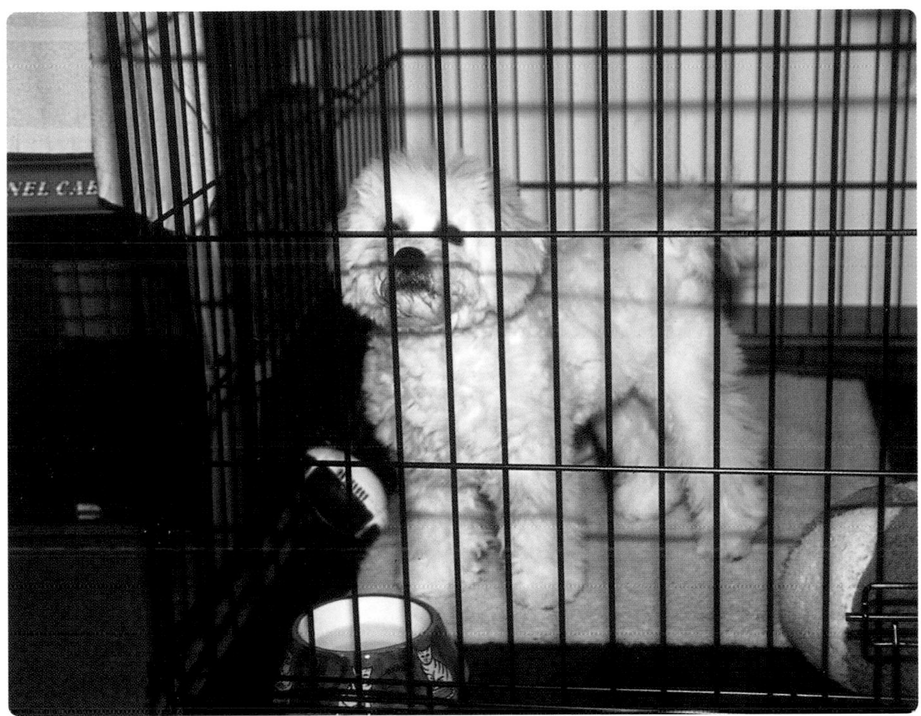

reinforce the barking. Your puppy will very quickly learn to "voice" every single complaint he may have. This is not only annoying, but you will never be able to determine if there really is a need to go outside.

Naturally, the length of time that the young puppy will be able to contain himself must be taken into consideration. Two or three hours in the crate are the maximum in the beginning, except at night when the entire household is quiet and dark. The length of time can be increased as the puppy grows older. If you ignore him when he cries to come out and only let him out when he is being quiet, he will eventually understand that theatrics will not result in liberation. Some dogs are more adamant about their dislike of confinement. There are safe methods of dealing with dogs that are determined to win these battles of will and we will deal with some of them later in Chapter 5.

Helpful Hints

It's not necessary to dash out and buy a new crate every few weeks to accommodate your puppy's rapid growth spurts. Simply cut a piece of plywood to partition off the excess space in the adult-size crate and move it back as needed. Your puppy will be well on his way to being housebroken long before you have lost the need for the partition.

Paper Training

If you find it necessary to be away from home all day, you can still successfully housebreak your dog. While you cannot leave your puppy or dog in a crate all day, do not make the mistake of allowing him to roam the house or even a large room at will. Begin housebreaking your dog by placing newspapers or puppy housebreaking pads in an area that is easily accessible to him. Confine the puppy to a small room or an area of the house partitioned with baby gates and cover the floor with newspaper or puppy pads. Although newspapers involve no extra cost, they will get both your white puppy and the area in which he is confined dirty with newsprint smudges. They also don't always absorb what the puppy has to offer. Housebreaking pads on the other hand are absorbent, lined to prevent leaks, and some are treated with an attractant to lure your puppy to them when he needs to eliminate. Make your dog's special area large enough so that he will not have to relieve himself next to his bed, food, or water. You will soon find he will be inclined to use one particular spot of the area to perform his bowel and bladder functions. When you are home, you must take the dog to this exact spot to eliminate at the appropriate time. If you consistently take your dog to the same spot, you will reinforce the habit of going there for that purpose.

Socialization

All dogs must learn to get along well with people, but not every dog is going to love every stranger that comes his way. Fortunately, very few Bichons dislike people. There is an occasional exception to that rule, but the fault almost always lies with the humans that the Bichon has lived with.

Your Bichon must understand that humans lay down the rules and regulations in our society and that he must abide by those rules. Sound temperament enables a dog to do this. While sound temperament is the product of both heredity and environment, poor treatment and lack of socialization can ruin the best temperament a dog might possibly inherit. A dog that has inherited a bad temperament is a nuisance at best and downright dangerous at worst.

A dog with a sound temperament can be introduced to the unending complications and stresses of modern living and survive them all. Children are particularly good at assisting their dogs to learn household rules and to cope with what has become our very modern and complex lifestyle. Puppies born or raised in homes with supervised children seem particularly good at adapting themselves to new environments. Children's giggles and laughter help developing puppies to become accustomed to different tones and inflections of voice. Because of their size, children seem less overwhelming to puppies. Perhaps these are just some of the reasons why puppies and children seem to develop such an affinity for each other.

Breed Needs

To assist socialization, your dog should go everywhere with you—the post office, park, beach, and shopping mall—wherever. This applies to puppies as well, once shots are current. The more people your dog meets, the better socialized he will become.

Socialization is a process that begins when the puppy is born and must continue when the dog arrives at your home and throughout the rest of your dog's life with you. A dog may be very happy and well behaved at home with you and your family, but if socialization is not continued, that sunny disposition will not extend outside your front door.

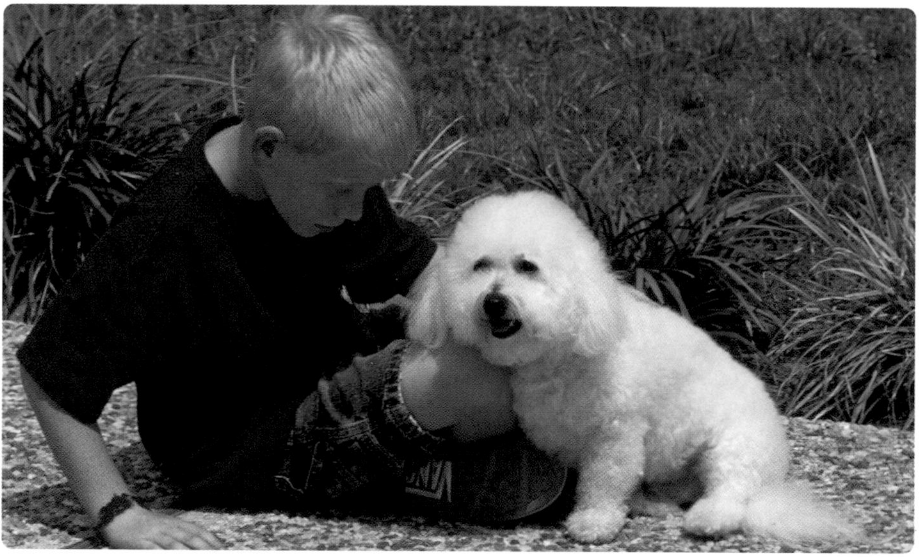

Never encourage aggressive behavior on the part of a puppy. It is more important for the dog to be able to become a good canine citizen and accept all he meets. Once you leave the confines of your home, everything you do will be an adventure for the puppy. Strangers will be met on the street, and it is up to you to teach your dog to meet them with a friendly attitude, as well as restraint.

Out on the Street

Other dogs and cats exist, and you and your dog will have to get used to it. You may never be able to teach your dog to love other four-footed creatures, but he must understand that all those other animals have just as much of a right to the streets and parks as he does.

There is nothing more irritating than to go through all the effort of responsibly training your dog only to have him harassed by an out-of-control and off-leash bully. If an off-leash dog approaches you and your dog, do not stop to let the two get acquainted! You do not know what the other dog's intentions are, and you could easily wind up in the middle of a dogfight. Continue walking without acknowledging the presence of the intruder and do your best to keep your dog from doing so. Usually, off-leash dogs are most aggressive when they are defending their own turf. If it is you and your dog that are on the stranger's turf, the best advice is to exit the area as quickly as you can.

Even people who love dogs aren't particularly pleased to have a strange dog come galloping headlong down the street and fling himself at them. Granted, the dog may be exhibiting his joy and his love for the world, but the stranger receiving the greeting doesn't know that.

Teach your dog to practice his good manners when meeting others. Carry treats with you when you go out. Practice the sit command by making your dog sit and wait to get petted when he meets someone. If your puppy backs off from a stranger, give the person one of the snacks and have that person offer it to your puppy. Insist your young dog be amenable to the attention of any strangers of whom you approve, regardless of sex, age, or race.

Once your dog learns to accept people outside of his family, he can begin to form friendships and establish trust. This will make everyday life with your dog a pleasant experience.

Puppy Behavior Problems

It must be completely understood that everything that happens to a puppy from the first minute he enters his new home is brand new. Your puppy's mind is a blank slate and you are responsible for everything that is written on it, be it good, bad, or indifferent. So make sure that everything that gets written there is exactly what you intended. Erasing bad habits can prove to be much harder than writing something there in the first place.

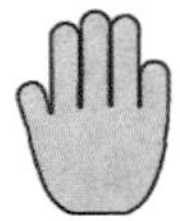

CAUTION

Even dogs that are trained for personal protection are taught to stand and be touched by a stranger if their owner gives the command. It is not up to your puppy to decide who he will or will not tolerate. You are in charge. You must call the shots.

You must also understand that dogs do not understand the concept of "sometimes," as in sometimes it is OK to get up on the furniture, sometimes it is not. Sometimes it is okay to nip at your hand and sometimes it is not. With dogs, it is okay or it isn't. If you like snuggling on the sofa with your Bichon on a cold winter evening but don't want him on the furniture at other times, he won't understand the difference. It's a black-and-white dog's world. Do not let your puppy do anything that you do not want him to do for the rest of the time you are living together.

Normal Behavior vs. Real Problems

Certain behaviors that all puppies learn from their littermates are perfectly normal. Growling, wrestling, digging, chewing, nipping, and whining when left alone are things that all puppies do. How you handle them will determine whether or not they become real problems.

Remember, it is a black-and-white world for your puppy. He growled and nipped at his brothers and sisters in the early days of his life, so it is perfectly normal for him to continue to do so when he leaves the nest. This action does not represent aggressive behavior. However, it can become a problem when he learns that growling or snapping will get him his way.

The same goes for whining when left alone. He must be taught that this is not acceptable—*ever.* Allowing your puppy out of his crate or into the other room when he whines simply teaches him that whining or howling is the method by which he can get what he wants. It also sets the stage for neurotic behavior and separation anxiety.

Chapter Five

Living with a Bichon Frise

Bichons will pretty much get along with anyone willing to get along with them. They are just as happy living in a Manhattan penthouse as they are on an Iowa farm. I know of Bichons that live in both environments and I can assure you they adjust to city life just as easily as they do living in the country. Bichons do fit in just about anywhere because they are small enough not to need a Land Rover to be hauled around in, yet big enough so that they're not blown two counties away by the first brisk wind that comes along. A Bichon can give his owner unfailing cheerfulness and devotion and, although this may sound surprising, the Bichon can also make a very good little watchdog.

The Bichon Frise can be an ideal family pet in that the breed is large enough to easily accompany the more active members of the family on hikes and participate in most games. At the same time a Bichon is small enough to be a companion to the smaller, gentler, or less physically active members of the household. However, coat care and upkeep is a strong consideration.

Coat Care

As appealing as a Bichon puppy or adult might be, this is a *white* dog that needs frequent bathing and constant coat care in order to maintain his look. To make matters worse, a Bichon is the eternal child and enjoys playing in the mud or burying himself in the sandbox as much as any human child would. And that, it should go without saying, wreaks havoc upon those fluffy teddy bear looks.

The Bichon is a long, coated breed that will only stay looking anything like a Bichon in so long as you are willing to keep him clean, brushed, and trimmed. You must either learn to trim little Pierre yourself (no easy task I assure you) or be willing to spend the necessary money to have the grooming and trimming done professionally. If you appreciate the look of the breed, understand that it will take some time and effort on your part to keep your dog looking that way.

Neglect of a Bichon's coat ensures matting that attracts debris and parasites. Quicker than you might guess it will become necessary to have the neglected Bichon shaved to the skin. What the average person doesn't realize is that the coats of the long-haired breeds serve as insulation against both heat and cold. Having your Bichon shaved to the skin once or twice a year isn't doing him a favor; it is making him even more uncomfortable than carrying around that felted coat. Personally speaking I have never been able to figure out why the person who neglects, then shaves, his coated dog doesn't just get a smooth-coated breed in the first place.

Few breeds are more versatile, amiable, or adaptable than the Bichon Frise. Don't overlook the breed's incredibly versatile history. Bichons have been pets of the nobility, seafarers, street urchins, and circus entertainers. With a history like that it should be obvious that the Bichon can fit into almost any caring and compatible household.

Breed Truths

You can rely upon your Bichon to let you know the doorbell has rung or someone is knocking at the door but at the same time, the breed is not one to drive you wild with constant and needless barking. Be forewarned, however, with all that said, once *you* welcome a stranger into your home, forget any thoughts of further protection. Bichons love company as much, if not more, than you do and they could care less that the company "just dropped in."

Bichons and Children

Bichons love well-mannered children and can enjoy most rough and tumble games with Junior as much as they would attending a tea party with the young lady of the house. The breed is neither too rough for the girls of the family nor too timid for the boys. A word of caution here, however—infants and very young children who have not yet learned how to handle animals should never be left unsupervised with a Bichon, especially a Bichon puppy.

An inexperienced child is far more apt to injure the Bichon than the other way around but it must be remembered that a dog of any breed protects himself with his teeth and untrained puppies and less patient seniors may use their teeth to ward off childish fingers inclined to put themselves in unwanted places.

Most breeders make an effort to expose their young puppies to children of various ages but occasionally this isn't possible for some reason or another and your puppy may never have seen any of these "miniature people" in his young life. First sighting of a child can be perplexing and frightening to an inexperienced puppy, especially so if the child rushes for or grabs at the puppy.

Once a good relationship has been established, it is amazing how well children and Bichons are able to communicate and bond with each other. In some primal way, without the use of words, they can express countless emotions, including devotion and trust in each other, that very few adults are privileged to enjoy.

Many parents believe that having a dog in their child's life teaches responsibility. Certainly this is true as long as the parent is there to teach the child just how dependent a dog really is on his owner. The parent must also be on hand to take control of situations that a child is incapable of handling.

CAUTION

When introducing a puppy that hasn't had any experience with children it is best to hold the puppy yourself. He will have you to rely on for protection and reassurance. Have the child sit on the floor while you do the same, still holding on to the puppy. If puppy and child seem compatible, allow the child to gently pet the puppy. Little by little you can share holding the puppy with the child and eventually allow the puppy to sit in the child's lap. Make it a gradual, easy process. Most Bichons will take to children with enthusiasm once they understand that the youngsters are not something strange or threatening.

Bichons and Other Pets

I have observed Bichons getting on famously with cats, rabbits, birds, and even some small exotic animals. A good deal depends upon the age at which the Bichon is introduced to other family pets. The younger your Bichon is, the more readily he will learn to accept even the strangest of resident pets. If done gradually and if the other pet doesn't overreact, this can be accomplished in a short time.

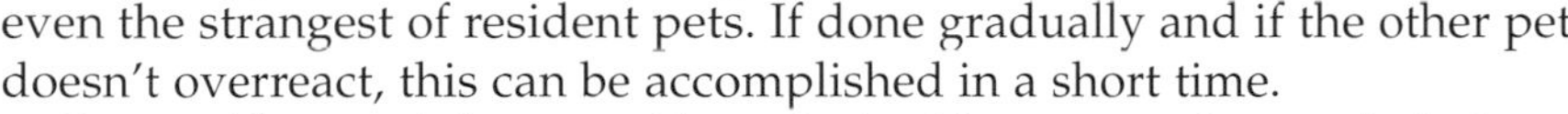

Be considerate of the pet with seniority. Young puppies can be holy terrors and may take great delight in chasing the family cat or harassing the old timer who wants nothing more than to be left alone to snooze in the afternoon sun. A reckless, rough-and-tumble puppy may not be as well received by pets with prior status as by you and your family.

The pets in residence have given you their all, sometimes for years, and all of a sudden they have to share the household and your affection with an intruder. Be considerate and allow those with seniority to get used to the changes.

All too often the established pet will be tethered or confined and the newcomer puppy will be allowed to nag and pester at will. It is the puppy that should be confined to his pen or wire crate. This allows the pet with seniority to inspect and make overtures to the young intruder slowly, without having to tolerate unwanted advances.

Little rodents or birds may represent toys to your Bichon and these toys just might wind up in his mouth. Save introductions of this kind until you get some sense of how your puppy or grown Bichon might approach the little critters.

Breed Needs

Your new Bichon puppy will have many things to learn when he becomes a part of your family, but the first and most important lesson is the meaning of the word "No!" He must understand that "No" means he must without question stop what he is doing immediately. Learning this lesson well could one day save your Bichon's life.

Living Quarters

The Bichon is not a breed to be shut away in a kennel or outdoor run with only occasional access to his owner's life and environment. That simply will not work. If your lifestyle doesn't accommodate the in-home companionship of a dog, you may well be served by another less needy breed. The very essence of the Bichon is in his sparkling personality and sensitive nature and the only way that can be fully developed is by regular human contact.

That does not mean that your Bichon must have a constant companion every hour of every day. There are times when for safety's (and sanity's!) sake Pierre can be placed in an area where he will be safe and also out from under foot. This can be a secure outdoor run in pleasant weather or a travel kennel in some quiet part of the house.

Since the Bichon is a lover of *all* humans he is not beyond accepting a ride in an automobile or an invitation to play, even if the invitation might come from a total stranger. Secure fences and closely latched doors and gates preclude that happening.

Destructive Behavior

It wouldn't be entirely surprising to hear that a Bichon who has been completely housebroken would abruptly forget all his manners in protest of suddenly being left alone too often or too long. Some Bichons will let you know they are not getting the attention they need by destroying household items. Invariably they'll choose a personal item belonging to their owner or some member of the family that they are particularly fond of. Although the owner might be inclined to think this is done out of spite, it is far more likely to be a case of the dog attempting to ingest the essence of the person he misses.

Regardless of why it is done, behavior of this nature should not be tolerated and attempting to correct it after the fact can be extremely difficult. Therefore, it is best to have a safe and secure area for your Bichon to stay while you are away. He will not be able to destroy furniture or items of clothing if he is not able to get to them. Nor will he able to soil his surroundings and then bound off to another part of the household to avoid having to deal with his misdeed.

None of this should be construed to mean that only those individuals who are home all day to cater to the whims of their dog could be a Bichon owner. We know many working people who are away most or a good part of the day whose Bichons are well-mannered and trustworthy when left home alone. The key here seems to be the *quality* rather than *quantity* of time spent with the pet. Morning or evening walks, grooming sessions, game time, and simply having your Bichon share your life when you are home is vital to the breed's personality development and attitude. Bichons like to be talked to and praised. The old adage, "No man is an island," needs to be expanded to include dogs—especially Bichons.

How About You?

The foregoing gives you somewhat of a capsulated idea of what life with the average Bichon might be like. Will all Bichons act and react in that exact manner? Probably not, but close. We're dealing with living, breathing creatures here that react to external influences like all other living creatures. What may affect puppy A might not even phase puppy B. But by and large,

BE PREPARED! Is a Bichon Frise Right for You?

The following is a list of questions that should be answered by anyone who is thinking about adding a Bichon Frise to his or her household. Anything other than answers in the affirmative indicate that serious consideration should be given before a final decision is made.

1. Does everyone in the household want a dog?
2. Is a Bichon the kind of dog that will suit the wants and needs of everyone in the household?
3. Is the person who will actually be responsible for the Bichon's day-to-day care (including brushing, health checks, and exercise) willing and able to do so?
4. If there are children in the home, are they old enough to understand what proper treatment of a dog like a Bichon entails?
5. Is there a safe, secure place for a Bichon to be kept when there is no one available to supervise him?
6. Are you able to afford professional grooming at least every three months or do you have the desire and ability to learn to do this yourself?
7. Have you considered the additional cost of Bichon ownership beyond the original purchase price? There are veterinary check ups, illnesses, food, and grooming supplies.
8. Do you have the time and temperament necessary to teach a Bichon all the household rules you expect him to obey?

Bichons are pretty easy to get along with, just as long as they are given ample opportunity to be with "their people."

A well-bred and well-trained Bichon has qualities that have made the breed an ideal family dog. You must understand, however, that the operative words are "well-bred and well-trained." Far too many would-be Bichon owners fulfill their dreams of Bichon ownership by rushing down to the local mall and buying the first puppy they see advertised as "100% pedigreed pure Bichon." They don't stop to consider the temperament and constitution of the parents or the amount of work that will be involved in creating a good canine citizen out of that curly mop of raw material.

Before dashing out to buy yourself one of these wind-up fluff balls, there are a number of important things you really need to do. First, think back on what your experience with pets of any kind has been. Did feeding the goldfish prove to be such a chore you had to call in assistance? Was refilling the wild bird feeder something that didn't get done more than once the entire winter?

Sit down and think very clearly about your personal lifestyle or that of your family. You may be single and a workaholic who is only home long

enough to change clothes before heading back to the office. Your family may be involved in so many activities that coming and going extends right around the clock.

None of these scenarios are conducive to raising and training a Bichon pup. The puppy that you bring into your home has no knowledge of household rules nor is he able to fend for himself while you or the family is elsewhere.

Once a dog enters your household he will be there all day, every day. He will rely entirely upon you for care and comfort. If getting a dog was your idea in the first place, don't rely upon someone else in the family to step in and help unless they have already volunteered to do so.

Kids in the family are always ready to promise, promise, and *promise* that not a day will go by without making Pierre their first priority. Don't depend on it. Any parent will tell you that a child's first priority can mean one thing today and entirely something else tomorrow.

If you enter into your commitment understanding that pets are more work than children are you'll do well! Your dog can't grab a snack out of the refrigerator when he's hungry. He has no burning desire to be toilet trained and could care less about cleaning up his own messes. Nor is he going to take dance classes or join the soccer team to bring down that energy level a few notches.

All that is up to you, you and only you! If you plan to hire someone to take care of all those things for you just so you can relax and have some ears to scratch—save yourself the time, aggravation, and money—get a stuffed toy or pet rock.

If you believe what you read in some of the "I Love My (enter breed here)" kinds of books written today, you would swear some breeds can do all that needs doing. Doggie braggers can have you believe that their breed is the one that can do it all, plus eliminate your need for an alarm system and teach your kids their multiplication tables on the side. Should you be naive enough to believe that such a breed exists, be warned—the Bichon Frise is *not* one of them!

If growing a few African Violets or giving a plant an occasional drink of water proved to be sheer drudgery, dog care is going to make you feel like an indentured servant! Potted plants shrivel up and disappear after a few weeks of neglect. When a Bichon is neglected he will eat your shoes and wet on the carpet. He doesn't do this out of spite; it's just his way out of boredom and proves lack of supervision.

In nature when little wolf cubs begin to venture away from the nest that their mother made for them they start looking for two important things—a pack leader and the pack rules and regulations that let them know what they can and cannot do. Surprisingly, and despite how much mankind has meddled in the transition of wolf to domesticated dog, the canine world's needs remain very much the same.

Just like his distant ancestor, a Bichon looks for a leader and wants to know what the pack's rules are. Since your pup does not reside in the great North Woods, guess who is elected to perform all the duties of the pack leader? If you guessed yourself, you are right on track. If you provide what your pup needs, you will have a great companion. If you don't, you will have more headaches than you'll ever want or need.

Home Alone

If you live alone, the ownership answer is simplified on the one hand, complicated on the other—you will be the sole care giver. But if you do live alone, you probably have to trudge off to Wall Street or to a movie lot each day so you can earn the money to keep little Pierre in dog biscuits. Who then, will sit and hold your white whirlwind's busy little paw? You will need someone to look in on the little angel while he's still a pup.

If you share your life with a significant other or an entire family, other opinions will have to be considered as well. Your significant other may not be remotely interested in having your twosome become a threesome.

In many households mothers, even working mothers, seem to win the daily drawing for "Who'll-take-care-of-Pierre-when-the-family's-away?" We all know that mothers are modern day Wonder Women but all too often they're saddled with all the responsibility of caring for the dog they really didn't want in the first place. The lady of your household might not be as keen as you are about adopting still another needy child. Do remember—*this was your idea!*

Don't forget about training. Bichons need a lot of it as youngsters. Training takes time and patience (with a very strong emphasis on the latter). This is something that should take place every day whether it happens before work, after work, or on the lunch break. It has to happen. Not feeling up to it doesn't count. Not only must you feel up to it, you must *be* up to it. By that I mean your state of mind will have a great deal to do with how well your training sessions go.

Losing patience and taking it out on your Bichon doesn't work. Bichons are extremely sensitive. Yell a little too loud at a Bichon and you'll see what I mean. A properly raised and educated Bichon understands and accepts correction but the breed absolutely does not tolerate abuse. If subjected to abusive treatment on a continuing basis even the best temperament in the world will be totally destroyed.

This doesn't mean a Bichon can't be corrected. On the contrary, a Bichon puppy has to start learning household rules from the very first day that he comes to your home. If the puppy is to believe you and learn to avoid certain behavior, the *"No!"* command has to mean *no* all the time—not just most of the time or when he decides he wants to respond.

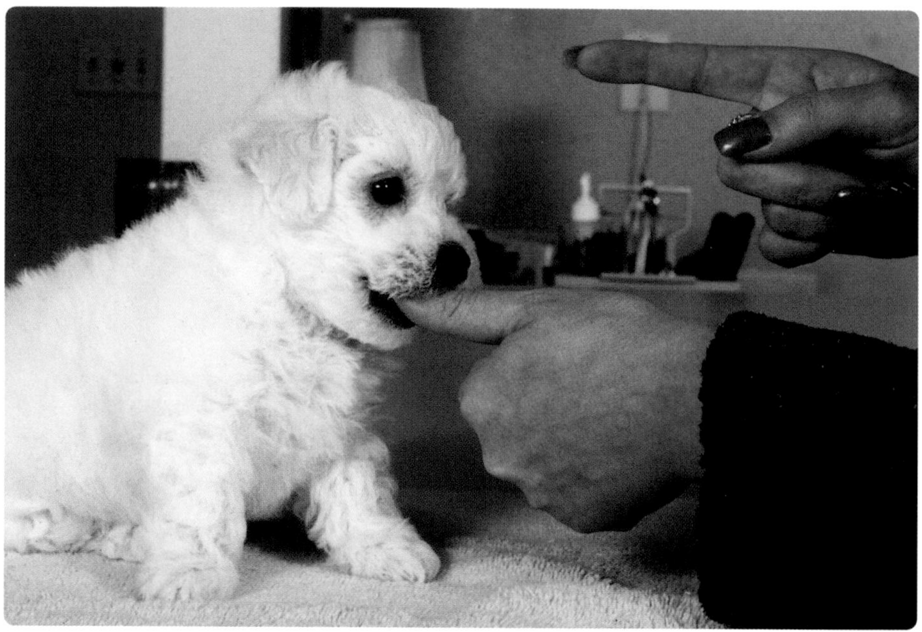

Problem Solving

What my parents assured me were "the best days of my life" were spent as an English Education major at Michigan State University. The battle hymn of the teaching staff at MSU at the time was quite simply, "If the learner hasn't learned, the teacher hasn't taught." Most schools of canine behavior are inclined to agree with that principle.

Bichons are smart and can learn quickly—if they are taught properly. Think of your Bichon's mind as an empty slate. If you want writing to appear there, you are going to have to do it, especially if you want the words to be those that you'll approve of.

At the same time, that doesn't mean that everything your Bichon does wrong reflects a flaw on your part. A dog comes equipped with a whole set of instinctual behaviors. Some of those behaviors are acceptable in human society, but a good many of them aren't and must be redirected.

But let's back up a bit. Let's go back to a few weeks after your Bichon was born. Individual breed characteristics aside, all dogs, whether wild or domesticated, are looking for two things when they leave the nest: a pack leader and the rules set down by the leader, by which all members of the pack must abide. Because Bichon puppies are cuddly and cute, a good many owners fail miserably in supplying these basic needs.

Instead, new owners immediately begin to respond to the cute little demands of the puppy. For example, a puppy quickly learns he will be allowed into the house because he is barking or whining at the door, not because he is *not* barking or whining. The grown dog scratches at the door to come in until the wood begins to wear away. In desperation, the owner allows the dog to enter. Pierre has learned an important lesson here—the quickest way to gain admittance is to start scratching a hole in the door.

Rather than allowing this unwanted "let me in" behavior to become established in the first place, you must develop a little in-and-out procedure that your Bichon understands. Before letting him in or out teach him he must first sit quietly. Then and only then will you open the door. Start this procedure the first time the two of you go out and you will be amazed at how rapidly he learns that sitting quietly at the door gets him just what he wanted.

It is important in situations of this kind to make sure your Bichon learns that the desired behavior has earned him what he wants. Once your dog has accomplished the acceptable behavior, praise him and then allow him to enter.

If the young puppy cannot find his pack leader in his owner, he can easily assume the role of pack leader himself. If there are no rules imposed, he learns to make his own rules. And, unfortunately, the unaware owner continually reinforces the puppy's decision to be in charge by allowing negative situations to take place.

Owners of large dogs who allow this behavior to develop can create a dangerous situation. However, just because the Bichon is not in the giant-dog category, the "I'm my own pack leader" Bichon can grow up to be a neurotic nuisance. Neither situation is an acceptable one.

The key to successful training lies in establishing the proper relationship between dog and owner. The owner or the owning family must be the pack leader and must provide the rules by which the Bichon abides without exception.

Problem Behavior

Adult Aggression

Most types of aggression can be dealt with and controlled as previously described (Chapter 4). In the extremely rare case of unprovoked aggression on the part of a Bichon, immediate measures should be taken to correct this highly unusual behavior for the breed. Since this is such untypical behavior, the problem could well be a physical ailment. The best course of action is to get a professional involved immediately—a veterinarian initially and if there does not seem to be a physical problem, seeking the council of a qualified trainer would be the next step.

In a good many cases, aggression can be the result of an effort to establish dominance or to be protective. Boundaries, both behavioral and territorial, are very important for dogs to learn. Being taught early on what he can and cannot do leaves the rare Bichon with aggressive inclinations no opportunity to decide how to behave. It is up to the owner to establish the boundaries by which his or her companion will live.

Absolutely no law-abiding citizen should have to endure being menaced by an aggressive dog. Granted, the Bichon is not a large dog and would not be as likely to do as much harm as would some of the larger breeds, but owners of all dogs must understand that there are many people who are afraid of any dog, and threatening behavior even on the part of the smallest of dogs can be terrifying for these people.

If a Bichon under six months of age snaps or bites, it is usually a strong indication of inherited bad temperament. Correcting or harnessing inherited bad temperament is a risky undertaking at best and usually leads to dire consequences at some point in the dog's life. Temperamentally untrustworthy puppies grow up to be temperamentally untrustworthy adults.

If the puppy was purchased from a breeder, he should be returned to the breeder without delay. If the puppy has not been obtained from a responsible source, I strongly advise discussing the next step with your veterinarian or dog behaviorist.

Separation Anxiety

Canine separation anxiety is a problem of a more serious nature than a dog not liking to be left alone. It is a neurological distress response to separation from the person to whom the dog is attached. Dogs so afflicted have a high degree of uncertainty of an outcome, or the probability of punishment. In dogs with this condition, the level of anxiety far outweighs the inciting circumstances.

Brain chemistry plays a major role in the development and progression of separation anxiety. It is important to understand that dogs with separation

FYI: Signs of Separation Anxiety

These symptoms can range from mild to severe.

- Distress vocalization: howling, barking, and whining
- Inappropriate elimination: urination, defecation
- Destructive behavior: chewing, digging
- Anorexia/"depression" or inactivity
- Psychosomatic/medical consequences: excessive licking of hair, pacing, circling
- Hyperattachment: excessive greeting behavior, constant pestering of owner
- Hyper salivation

anxiety are suffering and that they require behavioral management and medical intervention.

In the average U.S. veterinary practice, approximately one-third of canine patients exhibit one or more signs of separation anxiety. Fortunately the problem is a treatable disorder.

The condition is usually seen in younger dogs, especially when these pets are adopted from an animal shelter. It is not commonly seen in middle-aged dogs, although dogs that develop separation anxiety when they are young could well be at greater risk for recurrences later in life.

Separation anxiety is also common in older dogs. It is believed that as some animals age, lose their hearing and sight, they become more dependent on their owners, and become anxious when they are separated or even just out of sight

There are new drugs that have been approved to help relieve the high anxiety that separation creates for some dogs. They act on the dog in a manner similar to the calming effect of antidepressants on humans. These drugs can be obtained by prescription through your veterinarian. Although the drugs do not actually cure the problem, they relieve the symptoms to the extent that retraining can begin. It is *retraining* that is the operative word here.

Clomicalm (clomipramine hydrochloride) has proven especially effective in treating separation anxiety. The drug alters behavior by its action on neurotransmitter systems within the brain. Serotonin is a neurotransmitter that plays a significant role in fear and anxiety. Norepinephrine is involved with learning, memory, mood, arousal, and behavioral focus. Clomicalm blocks the uptake of both of these neurotransmitters in the brain. Increased levels of Serotonin reduces the distress the dog's fear and associated signs in dogs with separation anxiety. In some cases increased norepinephrine levels have been reported to stimulate the learning ability of some dogs, which may assist in the important behavior modification.

Effective treatment of canine separation anxiety involves both medical intervention and behavioral modification. Behavioral modification techniques are based on the principles of desensitization and counter-conditioning. This training is relatively simple and can in many cases be accomplished in a relatively short period of time.

When a dog suffers from separation anxiety, stern reprimands or punishment should never be resorted to, as it may actually increase anxiety. Having another dog present can often solve the anxiety problem quickly. Other dogs respond well to something as simple as having the radio or TV playing while the owner is gone.

It only makes sense that a dog that reacts to loneliness by being destructive should never be allowed to remain loose when you are gone. Some people think it cruel to confine their dog to an area or his crate, where he is not able to destroy things, but at the same time they think nothing of becoming furious and frightening the dog out of his wits when he has been free to be destructive. Reacting in a rage will only tend to enforce the dog's fear of being alone.

Regardless of the cause—loneliness or separation anxiety—owners who make their departures and returns monumental events compound the problem. Don't upset your dog before leaving by giving the poor fellow hugs and kisses like you are ready to take off on a year-long safari. Just go! When you return, don't make it a climax suitable for the theater screen. Some dogs love those dramatic returns and begin vocally requesting them the minute you walk out the door. Make leaving home and coming home as uneventful as possible or distract your dog by offering him a toy or treat before you leave. If he is happily occupied, the chances are he won't even notice you've gone.

Housebreaking Problems

The free-feeding method, leaving a constant supply of food for your dog so he can eat whenever he wants, is fine for some breeds of dogs, but I would not recommend it for Bichons. Bichons, particularly grown dogs, that are having problems getting the housebreaking message should only be fed at regular meal times and then confined until they can be taken to the place where they should eliminate.

Leg Lifting

This may be confusing to new dog owners, but when a male marks his turf, it has absolutely nothing to do with whether or not he is housebroken. Adult males have a natural instinct to lift their legs and urinate to "mark" their home territory. Home territory to a dog includes everything the two of you own—furniture, drapes, doorways, and bedspreads—nothing is sacred. He is just making sure no intruding males get the mistaken notion that they can move in on his turf. The best thing to do is to interrupt this behavior as soon as you see him do it.

Small dogs can be more difficult to break of this habit than the larger breeds. Undoubtedly, a good part of the reason is that they can get into the habit of doing this before their behavior is noticed. Neutered males are far less apt to mark than their sexually complete brothers.

Wandering

By and large, Bichons are not wanderers, but "boys will be boys" and even the most loving and obedient Bichon boy will pay heed to nature's call and wander off up the hill to seek the attention of the neighborhood femme fatale. Females are ready to breed twice a year—a male is ready any time and will shop around to see if there are any ladies-in-waiting. Neutering can help solve the wandering problem, but there is absolutely no better insurance against the wanderings of the canine lothario than a securely fenced yard.

Chewing

All dogs chew and the Bichon is no exception. Dogs chew for a whole lot of reasons. To begin with, dogs do everything with their mouths that we do with our hands. We humans, who should know better, do some terribly destructive things to relieve tension and escape from anxiety or frustration. Smoking cigarettes or compulsive eating are not exactly health measures, yet we continue to do them.

Your Bichon may chew to relieve anxiety and stress. Dogs that aren't given sufficient exercise use up some of that energy by chewing. Puppies experiment by chewing. They test everything they come across to see what it is, what it tastes like, and what it's made of. They chew to relieve the pressure of those tiny new teeth trying to burst their way through the gums. Chewing is good when it is done on a bone or a safe chew toy, but bad when the chewing takes place on the corner of your new coffee table or oriental rug.

Giving your Bichon things to occupy his time and taking him with you when you run errands or take short trips helps to keep those canine minds interested and active. There are very few dogs who are willing to sit around day after day, with absolutely nothing to do, and who won't eventually pick up something to gnaw on while they're relieving that boredom.

If you know your dog is inclined to chew and you leave him in the living room when you go to the movies, expect him to have obliged your negligence. If, on the other hand, he is tucked safely away in his crate or his own small area, with something to occupy his jaws, you can come home without fear that the entire encyclopedia set has been digested.

Jumping Up

As much as most of us like dogs and really don't mind their jumping up on us for joy some of the time, there are other times when it is not appropriate for them to do so. The problem is that dogs don't understand that it is okay to jump up on you when you are wearing jeans, but not so okay when you are all dolled-up and waiting for your date to arrive or you are on your way to the church social. Also, some people are terrified of dogs and the last thing in the world they want is to have Pierre leaping all over them. For all of these reasons and more, dogs must be taught not to jump up on anyone—ever—not even when they are puppies.

If Pierre comes bounding up to greet you and plants his feet on you for a love pat, push those paws down and command, *"Off!"* Just as soon as all four of the dog's feet are on the ground, praise him lavishly.

Remember to use only the *"Off"* command and no other. Don't say *"Down"* unless you actually want your dog to lie down. Don't try *"No"* one time and *"Scoot"* the next. Success depends upon your dog associating the behavior with the word.

One of the problems you may face is that some people will ignore your wishes and say, "Oh, I don't mind, I have dogs of my own. I love them all." They are trying to be nice, but nevertheless they are making your training job more difficult. You'll have to be direct about this situation and simply tell the person that you appreciate their kindness but that you are in the process of trying to teach the dog not to jump up on people. I'm sure they'll understand and respect your wishes.

The "no-jumping-up" rule has to apply to everyone in the family as well. It's difficult for a dog to determine who doesn't mind and when the behavior is acceptable, and because it is something that dogs like to do, the lesson will take forever to get across if everyone in the household doesn't cooperate.

Digging

There's hardly a dog I know that doesn't like to dig. Most dogs do it outdoors, but I've even known some that like nothing better than digging their way through a down comforter or sofa cushion. The urge to dig is just a dog being a dog, but destructiveness is something that has to be dealt with quickly and in no uncertain terms. Again, avoidance and *immediate* correction come into play here.

Outdoor digging is harmless unless it is in the middle of the lawn or in your newly planted flowerbed. When this is the case, you'll be glad that the *"No"* command was one of the first lessons you taught your Bichon. The Bichon that minds extremely well may be content to leave it at that. However, a lot of other dogs may simply move on to another part of the flowerbed or lawn and start digging again.

Giving your Bichon his own "sandbox" could be the answer. To get the dog digging in his own place the first time, bury a bone or special treat there. You may even have to help Pierre find the buried treasure a time or two, but most dogs get the idea in a hurry and the problem may be solved.

Some dogs, however, are a little more determined than that. The only cure for the problem in this case may be keeping a watchful eye on your Bichon when you are together and, when you can't be watching, keeping the dog away from the area you do not want excavated.

Sexual Behavior

Male Bichons, in some cases even those that have been sexually altered, may mount people's legs or even inanimate objects. It can originate as a sexual urge or as an attempt to dominate. At any rate, it must be discouraged at the dog's first attempts to do so. Owners will often think it's cute when a puppy does this, but they live to regret not curbing the desire to mount when it becomes a frequent embarrassment or even a danger to the elderly or small children. Stopping this behavior immediately is the best way to avoid problems later on.

Summary

There are seldom hard and fast answers that can be applied across the board to resolve behavior problems for all dogs. Understanding the cause of a problem is the first step in correcting it. Then, too, it is important for the trainer to understand how important it is to avoid bad habits being established in the first place. Should the bad habit cycle already have started, there is no substitute for positive reinforcement of good behavior.

Communicating with Your Bichon Frise

Voice After thousands of years as a domesticated animal, dogs in general are quite capable of interpreting the nature of what we are trying to say through our tone of voice, the volume with which we speak, and the inflection in our words. The Bichon's long history as a household companion makes him especially attuned to these voice nuances. Regardless of what language you are speaking, dogs understand whether you are speaking to them in a happy, sad or angry manner. In addition to being able to pick up the subtleties of how we are saying our words, dogs are also believed to be capable of understanding hundreds of words as well as being able to pick out certain words when strung together in a sentence and make sense of what has been said. However, it can appear, at times, that the Bichon doesn't understand anything you've told him, particularly when you are scolding him. He appears to be totally crushed by what you are saying, to the point that you might wonder if even harsh words have been too great a punishment. Yet, with all the dramatic response to your scolding, very shortly he will repeat the action for which he was scolded. I do believe that some Bichons overreact to tone or volume of voice and disconnect with what the scolding was about. A Bichon will hear and understand what you are saying far more quickly if you use positive, reward-based training techniques.

Hands Much of the way in which dogs communicate with each other is through body language. It is believed that dogs are very visual learners, the Bichon included. What this means to you is that you may find that, when you are training, your puppy or adult will excel at learning hand signals. You will be able to link a hand signal with a behavior quite easily. The advantage of teaching your Bichon basic commands using hand signals is that you can show anyone of any age how to give the hand signals, and your Bichon will understand what he is being told. With voice commands, a "*Sit*" may sound quite different coming from a high-pitched toddler than a deep-toned man—and the Bichon will pick up on these tonal differences, possibly causing confusion. With hand signals, you will not find this confusion.

Facial Expressions If you watch your Bichon as you are talking to him, it's very obvious that he has facial expressions: he will relax and tighten his eyes, shift ear positions, open and close his mouth, etc. It's not just an old saying that you can tell what your Bichon is thinking by "reading" his facial expressions. Additionally, Bichons can recognize people's facial expressions (remember, they're visual learners) and, in fact, have been known to mimic a human's smile (which is not a dog behavior at all). When working to communicate with your dog, many trainers recommend combining appropriate facial expressions with rewards to help your Bichon understand what you are training him to do. Smiling when you're pleased comes naturally to some people, but is more difficult for others. (An angry look and a *"No!"* can also get the message across much better than simply saying *"No!"*)

Body Movement

As noted previously, dogs communicate by using their bodies. Greeting behaviors among domestic dogs are highly ritualized, making them recognizable by all sizes, types, breeds, and mixes of dogs, no matter where in the world they have been raised. Using your body to communicate your joy or your displeasure can also help your Bichon to understand what you are trying to communicate to him. Again, some owners have a harder time unleashing the inner thespian when training their dogs, and other owners sometimes are too demonstrative (which can overwhelm a more timid dog). If your body language matches what you are trying to communicate to your dog, you will find that your Bichon has an easier time understanding your message. NOTE: Threatening body language should never be used when working with dogs—its only result is to create fear and distrust.

Scents

Dogs can paint a picture in their minds from what they smell. The scent of urine on a telephone pole, to the Bichon, is a news report on another dog: "male, intact, large breed, owner of the block or older male, neutered, looking for a good playmate." The Bichon's ability to detect smells tells him much more about you than you can ever imagine. Dogs can detect changes in our chemical makeup and are capable of smelling a seizure 30 minutes before it occurs, and scenting out the early stages of several different types of cancer. It would be no surprise to many Bichon owners if it were determined that Bichons could actually scent out our mood changes, too. So, though we can't purposefully communicate to our Bichons using scents, the Bichon may possibly have a greater understanding of our subconscious communications through the breed's incredible sense of smell.

Chapter Six

Health and Nutrition

The happy, healthy Bichon puppy you brought into your home got that way because his breeder gave him everything he needed to develop to his full potential. He was fed a healthful, balanced diet and given proper veterinary attention. Now it's up to you to continue that care, ensuring your puppy grows to be a healthy adult dog.

Diet

A balanced diet is a necessity for proper canine health. Different breeds require different approaches to nutrition—a Great Dane for example, will have different calorie requirements than your Bichon. The selection of dog foods and supplements available at grocery and pet stores can be overwhelming, so before you purchase food for your pup, discuss his dietary needs with your breeder. He can describe the types and brands of foods your puppy has been eating and explain why he feels they are best for your Bichon.

All dog foods are not the same. Foods differ in the ingredients used to reach the minimum daily requirements for dogs as established by the FDA, so read labels carefully. Manufacturers are required by law to list ingredients by weight in descending order.

Packaged dog foods come in three basic forms: dry kibble, canned, and semi-moist. Quality dry food contains all the nutrients a healthy dog needs and is the most economical over the long run. Chewing dry food also helps prevent tartar buildup on the teeth. Mixing a bit of canned food with a dry kibble will tempt a finicky Bichon. Semi-moist foods, while palatable, are more expensive than dry and contain many unnecessary additives.

Premium and Prescription Diets

These usually high-quality foods are available in specialty shops and from your veterinarian. While more expensive than the commercial type dog foods available in pet emporiums and supermarkets, premium foods are more consistent in quality and are often easier to digest. Prescription diets are specially formulated to avoid exacerbating certain health conditions such as diabetes.

Commercial Diets

Commercial diets are those foods widely available in supermarkets and pet stores. They can be dry or moist. Most national name-brand foods are included in this category and provide adequate to good nutrition for your Bichon. Check the label on these foods carefully as the price does not always correspond to the quality and quantity of ingredients.

Helpful Hints

Your Bichon doesn't need to snack all day long, so only offer treats in moderation or save them for training. You puppy will be healthier for it!

Life Stage Formulas

Your dog will have different nutritional requirements at different points in his development. Many dog foods are specially formulated for different life stages.

Puppy formulas, as the name indicates, are created for the needs of growing puppies. Adult formulas come in many varieties. Your Bichon should be fed what is appropriate for both his age and activity level. Your vet and breeder can help you decide which to use. Senior diets are designed for the older dog. Some simply reduce fat and calories to compensate for decreased activity; better types reduce salt and adjust protein levels to make them easier on a dog's metabolism. Active older dogs may do better on an adult maintenance diet. Adult Bichons do not require the same percentage of protein in their diets as growing puppies. This is particularly true in hot summer weather. Excessive protein at that time of the year can cause severe itching; the dog can scratch or chew at "hot spots," breaking the skin.

FYI: Inoculations

Most breeders give their puppies at least one, if not two, inoculations before the puppies leave for their new homes. Complete immunity comes only after the complete series of inoculations is given, so make sure your Bichon receives his at the prescribed intervals.

Also, most boarding kennels and training groups will not accept your dog if you cannot furnish copies of his immunization record or if the inoculations are not completed or up to date. This requirement is enforced to protect the other dogs that are on the premises.

Obesity

Without a doubt one of the most frequent health problems seen by veterinarians is obesity, a condition usually caused by overfeeding, and which can easily affect the adult and senior Bichon. An overweight dog is susceptible to diabetes and heart disease, as well as joint problems. Feeding a large amount once daily will not cut your dog's calorie count. It is better to feed a small amount twice daily and reduce the number of calories per day. Keep in mind that treats add to your Bichon's calorie count and his weight.

Health Care

It is important to establish a weekly health care routine for your Bichon. Maintaining this schedule will prevent escalation of serious problems that may take expensive veterinary attention.

Helpful Hints

Most breeders recommend that puppies should be at least one year of age before getting their first rabies shot. Thereafter, give rabies inoculations as required, but *never* any less than two weeks before or after any other vaccine.

Vaccines

Diseases that once were fatal to almost all infected dogs are now very effectively dealt with through the use of vaccines. Vaccines introduce a minute amount of a disease into your Bichon's system so that he can build up an immune response to the disease. Subsequently, the dog will be able to ward off the disease should he be exposed at a later date. The recommended age for inoculation and the timing of the shots may vary from one veterinarian to another, so discuss these issues with both your breeder and your own veterinarian.

The danger of your Bichon being infected with distemper, hepatitis, hard pad, leptospirosis, or the extremely virulent parvovirus is unlikely just so long as the dog is properly inoculated and the recommended series of booster shots are given.

Cases of rabies among dogs are practically unheard of in the United States, but dogs that come in contact with wild animals of any kind can be at risk if not properly immunized. Rats, squirrels, rabbits, and many other small rodents can carry rabies, so it is important to have your dog immunized.

On rare occasions an immunized dog may not develop full immunity against some infectious diseases. Therefore it is important to have the ability to detect signs of these illnesses in case your Bichon is one of the few who are not completely immune and actually do develop the diseases.

Many puppies are extremely sensitive to the 5, 6 and 7 in 1 modified live vaccines for distemper, hepatitis, leptospirosis, parainfluenza and parvo virus (DHLPP). Some get very ill within two or three days of receiving the vaccines, others a couple of weeks later. Seizures and/or symptoms of hypothyroidism, liver and kidney problems, and heart complications may show up several years after receiving the vaccines. As a result, a good many breeders are recommending separate shots over a graduated period of time. Discuss this with your breeder and insist your veterinarian follow those recommendations to the letter.

Canine Diseases

Canine Parvovirus

This particularly infectious gastrointestinal disease is commonly referred to as "parvo." It can be contracted by direct contact or by being exposed to areas in which infected dogs have been housed. It is particularly fatal to puppies. Symptoms include acute diarrhea, often bloody, with yellow or gray colored stools. Soaring fevers, sometimes as high as 106 degrees, are not uncommon, particularly in puppies. Death can follow as quickly as one to three days after first symptoms appear. Early treatment is critical.

Canine Virus Distemper

The first sign of this very serious and often fatal disease is usually an extremely high fever. Mortality among puppies and adults that have not been immunized is extremely high. Loss of appetite, diarrhea, and blood in the stools, followed by dehydration, are other possible signs. Respiratory infections of all kinds are apt to accompany these conditions.

Hardpad

Hardpad often accompanies distemper and is considered to be a secondary infection, the symptom of which includes hardening of the pads of the dog's feet. The virus eventually attacks the central nervous system causing convulsions and encephalitis.

Infectious Hepatitis

Canine infectious hepatitis is a liver infection of extreme virulence. The virus eventually affects other parts of the body with varying degrees of intensity. The infected dog can run an entire range of reactions from listlessness, loss of appetite, and watery eyes to violent trembling, labored breathing, vomiting, and extreme thirst. Infection normally occurs through exposure to the urine of animals infected with the disease.

Leptospirosis

This bacterial disease is contracted by direct exposure to the urine of an infected animal. "Lepto" can affect both humans and animals, and can be fatal to both. Rapidly fluctuating temperatures, total loss of maneuverability, bleeding gums, and bloody diarrhea are all signs.

Rabies

Most often contracted through a bite from an infected animal, the rabies virus affects the central nervous system through inflammation of the spinal cord. In many cases, the animal exhibits unusual aggression and personality changes, as well as symptoms typical of other infectious diseases already described. Symptoms may not be as quick to appear or as detectable as in other diseases because they often resemble the symptoms of other less virulent diseases.

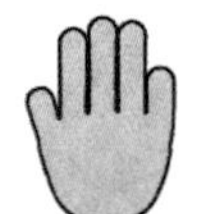

CAUTION

If you or your dog is bitten by an animal suspected of being rabid, seek immediate medical attention and contact the appropriate animal control agents.

Kennel Cough

Kennel cough, or bordatella, is similar to a mild case of the flu. While highly infectious, it is actually not a serious disease. Infected dogs act and eat normally, but develop a persistent, wrenching cough. It is highly contagious and easily passed from one dog to another through casual contact.

In severe cases antibiotics are prescribed to prevent secondary infections such as pneumonia. An intranasal vaccine is available, which provides immunity.

If your Bichon frequents a dog park or will be boarding at a kennel it's smart to vaccinate against kennel cough. Most boarding kennels now insist upon proof of immunization before they will accept a dog for boarding.

The Great Vaccination Debate

In all parts of the world debates rage over whether a dog should or should not continue to receive "booster shots" against infectious diseases on an annual basis.

Those opposed to booster shots cite occurrences of chronic health problems, sterility, and aborted litters as a result of over-administration of the vaccines. Those in favor argue that negative outcomes represent just a small percentage of the vaccinated population and the benefits far outweigh the risks.

There does, however, seem to be growing agreement that vaccines have a longer term of effectiveness than previously believed. A two- or three-year interval between the first shots and revaccination is now considered entirely appropriate.

There are no legal requirements regarding vaccinating your Bichon against any of the communicable diseases other than rabies. The rabies vaccine is not without risk in isolated cases, but the possibility of a negative reaction is far outweighed by the consequences of contracting the disease. Rabies can be transmitted to humans and it can be fatal. It is always fatal to dogs.

It is extremely important that you keep your dog's rabies inoculations current and that you have the tag issued by your veterinarian attached to your dog's collar. If your dog should ever bite someone you must be able to offer proof of current rabies inoculation. If not, your dog may, by law, be held in quarantine for a considerable length of time to determine the possibility of rabies infection.

Parasites—Inside and Out

Parasitic invasions can take place both internally and externally. Cleanliness, regular grooming, and biannual stool examinations by your veterinarian can help prevent infestations, but do not be upset or surprised to find that, despite your best efforts, your Bichon has become host to these nasty creatures.

External Parasites

External parasites are those that make their home on your pet's fur or skin.

Fleas Regardless of how meticulous you are in making sure Pierre stays clean and well groomed, you are bound to run into a flea problem at one time or another. Fleas exist almost everywhere and live for blood. They are usually found behind the shoulder blades and neck, and around the tail area.

There is no such thing as "one flea." If you find one, there are hundreds, even thousands lurking inside and outside your home. A flea bath for your Bichon is not going to solve the problem.

Fleas do not live on your dog, they simply feast there. Their home is in your carpeting, the grass in your yard, and in the brush along walking trails in gardens and parks. Cats with outdoor access can compound this already difficult problem by attracting fleas on their neighborhood patrols and bringing them back home. When fleas hop onto your dog for dinner, their biting will cause him to scratch. Bichons are particularly sensitive to fleas and their scratching can rupture the skin causing weeping sores or "hot spots."

Helpful Hints

Fleas act as carriers of the tapeworm eggs, so if your Bichon has fleas he will almost invariably have tapeworms. When a dog swallows a flea, the tapeworm eggs grow in the dog's intestines. For more on tapeworms, see page 84.

Because of the breed's sensitivity, it is best to discuss treatment options with your veterinarian. Herbal remedies, including brewer's yeast and garlic (home pressed and commercial pills), menthol, eucalyptus, and citronella can help as will pills and topical treatments. After discussing the benefits of these products with your veterinarian, following consistent recommended dosages can pretty well solve your flea problem.

Commercial services that do home spraying to exterminate flea problems can be successful but come with a price. Your home must be vacated and kept closed for several hours following the spraying. Some services now use nontoxic treatments; it's in both your and your Bichon's best interest to seek out these companies.

Lice Well-cared-for Bichons seldom encounter a problem with lice, as the parasites are spread by direct contact. A dog must spend time with another animal that has lice or be groomed with a contaminated brush or comb to pick them up.

To rid your Bichon of lice, you'll have to bathe him with an insecticidal shampoo every week until the problem is resolved. Lice live and breed exclusively on the dog itself so it is not necessary to treat the area in which the dog lives.

Ticks Ticks gorge themselves on the dog's blood and then find a dark little corner to raise a "family" that can consist of thousands of offspring at a time! Like fleas, they develop in stages—eggs, larva, nymph, and adult. If you live near a wooded area, you are bound to run across the occasional tick. In fact, your Bichon can pick one up simply by running through damp or shaded grass.

Ticks are usually found around the head and ears. Your Bichon's long hair provides plenty of camouflage, so check for small bumps on the skin. Parting the Bichon's coat and brushing in layers as described in Chapter 8 will make it easier to ferret out these little creatures.

A good many of the insect growth regulators that control fleas are now manufactured to combat the tick problem as well. These topically applied products are very effective and can keep your Bichon tick-free even in areas where there is a severe problem.

Helpful Hints

Tick Removal

The best method of removing a tick is to "smother" the tick by covering it in mineral oil. This causes the tick to release the fishhook-like barbs that it has inserted into the skin of your dog. Press down on either side of the tick with tweezers, squeeze the skin surrounding the tick tightly, and grasp the head, lifting the tick up and out. Immediately wrap the tick in toilet tissue, drop it into the toilet, and flush. Wash your hands with a disinfectant soap when you have finished.

Internal Parasites

Internal parasites represent much more of a danger to the health and well-being of your Bichon than their external cousins. This is especially true of young puppies as they can genuinely interfere with their growth and development by depleting the nutrients that are vital to healthy growth.

Roundworms These common pests are usually passed out of the system by adult dogs, but can seriously impair the growth and development of puppies. Roundworms are transmitted from mother to puppies; therefore responsible breeders make sure their females are free of worms before they are ever bred. The coats of puppies affected by roundworms are usually dull looking and the puppy itself is thin in appearance with a potbelly.

Infested puppies begin passing worm eggs at about seven weeks of age. Stool samples easily detect this parasite and veterinary treatment can entirely eliminate the problem.

Tapeworms Tapeworms are transmitted to dogs that ingest fleas (fleas eat tapeworm eggs). A small rice-like segment of the worm is often found crawling around the dog's anus or in the stool just after the dog has relieved himself. Periodic stool examinations done by your veterinarian can determine the presence of tapeworms. There are medications your veterinarian can administer that quickly and completely eliminate the problem.

Heartworms Mosquitoes carry the larvae of this worm and transmit them to your dog. Dogs are the only mammals that are commonly affected and the condition is most prevalent in warmer climates. Heartworms live in the chambers of a dog's heart and lungs. Heartworms can be prevented with oral medications, but your veterinarian must first conduct a blood test to see if heartworms are present.

Whipworms and hookworms These two worms can only be detected by microscopic examination of the stool and each worm requires specific medication to ensure elimination. Dogs can pick up these worms by eating the feces of infected animals. Both types attach themselves to the skin of humans and animals and eventually burrow their way to the lining of the intestines. They

FYI: Mangy Mites

Mange Mites are the culprit behind the two types of mange: demodectic and sarcoptic. Only sarcoptic mange is communicable, and both respond well to treatment.

Demodectic mange (*Dernodex canis*) is believed to be present on practically all dogs without causing any harm. Only about one percent of dogs ever develop clinical symptoms. Dogs affected locally may lose the hair around their eyes and in small patches on the chest and forelegs. This can be easily treated by a veterinarian, but must not be neglected. On rare occasions, the local form can develop into the more severe generalized form, which affects the entire body.

Sarcoptic mange Sarcoptic mange (*Sarcoptes scabiei var canis*) is also known as scabies and causes loss of hair on the legs and ears or in patches over the entire body. A skin scraping by your veterinarian will identify the type of mange present and determine the best treatment. Regular medicated baths with products especially formulated for sarcoptic mange will normally eliminate the problem. This type of mange is passed on by direct contact with infected dogs and is highly contagious.

are seldom passed or seen. Often the signs of infestation include weight loss, progressive weakness, and diarrhea.

Breed Truths

Thanks to natural selection, the genetic problems that often plague purebred dogs rarely surface in their undomesticated cousins (such as the Dingo of Australia and the wild dogs of Africa). Genetically transmitted infirmities that interfere with the dog's ability to obtain food or escape from predators are quickly eliminated from the gene pool.

Genetic Disorders

Like all breeds of domesticated dogs, Bichons have their share of hereditary problems caused by their limited gene pool. This doesn't necessarily mean that your Bichon will be affected with one of these disorders, but you should have a clear understanding of the problems common to Bichons. Your breeder can fill you in on the genetic history of your Bichon and advise you of the measures he's taken to help prevent them. In addition, the Bichon Frise Club of America has a committee dedicated to determining the causes of genetic disorders in the breed and can supply literature that explains these problems and how to deal with them.

Orthopedic Disorders

Bichons are known to be subject to inherited orthopedic problems. The most common of these problems are patella luxation and hip dysplasia.

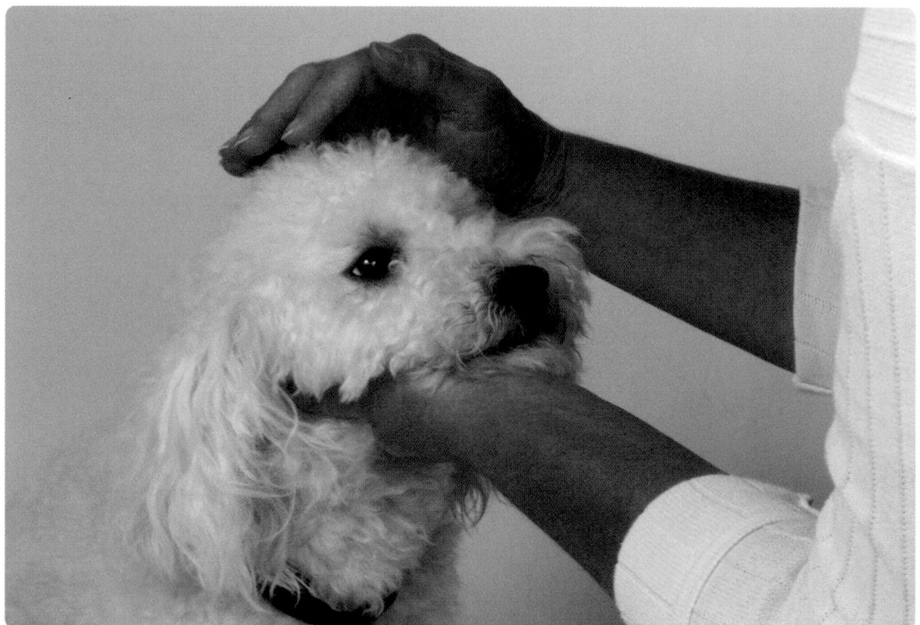

Patella luxation This condition is also commonly referred to as "slipping stifles" and is an abnormality of the knee joint (stifle), which leads to dislocation of the kneecap (patella). Normally the kneecap is located in a groove at the lower end of the thighbone and is held in this position by strong elastic ligaments. If the groove is insufficiently developed, the kneecap will leave its normal position and "slip" to one side or the other. The dog may exhibit an intermittent, but persistent, limp or have difficulty straightening out the knee. In some cases the dog may experience pain. Surgery may be required.

Hip dysplasia This is a developmental disease of the hip joint. Abnormal contours of one or both of the hip joints make the joint unstable. Dogs with displaysia show tenderness in the hip, walk with a limp or swaying gait, or experience difficulty when getting up. Symptoms vary from mild, temporary lameness to severe crippling. The light-bodied Bichon is seldom as severely afflicted as some of the heavier-bodied breeds. Surgery may be required.

Eye Problems

Secretion of tears and unsightly staining under the eyes can be a problem with white dogs. Have your veterinarian inspect your Bichon's eyes regularly to avoid problems early on.

Cataracts usually begin to form in the Bichon by age seven. The Canine Eye Registration Foundation (known as CERF) maintains a registry of dogs free from cataract troubles. Your Bichon should have several generations of his pedigree on that list. While fewer than 10 percent of Bichons have blinding cataracts, another 30–40 percent may be carriers. BFCA-sponsored research has determined that cataracts in Bichons are a recessive trait and research continues to find a DNA marker so that breeding stock can be tested for the gene prior to breeding.

Cataracts

A loss of the normal transparency of the lens of the eye, cataracts may affect one or both eyes and can involve the lens partially or completely. Some juvenile cataracts, which occur between the ages of one to six years, are not visible to the naked eye. Detection of early cataracts requires a special examination by a veterinary ophthalmologist—your personal veterinarian will most likely not be able to diagnose them until they are fully formed. Senile cataracts occur later in life. In cases where cataracts are complete and affect both eyes, blindness results. Surgery may or may not correct the problem and some Bichons suffer retinal detachment during surgery. Therefore it may be advisable to operate on only one eye at a time.

Corneal Dystrophy

This is a condition in which there appears to be a spot (or spots) on the surface of the eye. These usually do not affect the dog's eyesight.

Progressive Retinal Atrophy

This condition, commonly referred to as "PRA," is a degenerative disease of the retinal cells that progresses to blindness. It usually occurs in Bichons older than six years.

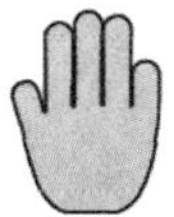

CAUTION

Immotile ciliary dyskinesia is a defect in the microscopic hairlike structures found in the respiratory tract, uterus, testicles, and Eustachian tube of the ear. This defect can cause chronic respiratory infections, sterility in both males and females, and loss of hearing. Appropriate antibiotic treatments are recommended to treat and prevent respiratory infections.

Bladder Problems

Bladder stones *(urolithiasis)* and bladder infections are considered one of the primary health issues in the Bichon Frise. Bladder stones is a condition where caculi are found in the urinary tract. *Struvite* stones are caused by infection and therefore are not considered to be inherited, though Bichons may be predisposed to them. Gingivitis, or gum disease, contributes to the problem, so it is vital to practice good dental hygiene. Infections in the mouth can cause germs to be spread to other organs or the bladder via the bloodstream. *Calcium oxalate* stones are inherited and, if not properly treated, may eventually develop a struvite coating, causing a misdiagnosis. For more information on Bichon bladder stones, see *www.bichon.org/stones.htm*.

Chapter Seven

Training and Activities

We obey laws because we know that if we don't, there are dire consequences for our transgressions. We have the ability to conceptualize punishment, but dogs do not.

Some canine behaviorists believe that all dogs' behavior comes from instinct. Others argue that dogs learn in as rational a manner as humans, or at least as human children do. Both schools of thought are able to offer convincing proof, and I believe that there is truth in both theories.

One cannot have lived with as many dogs as I have through the years and not observed both what is clearly instinctual behavior and what is obviously rational and learned. I do believe dogs learn to obey our "laws" in a manner that is similar, but different, from the way that we do. Because dogs learn differently, we must approach teaching them in a different manner.

Word Association

A specific word has no real meaning for a dog. A dog responds to what he associates the word with. For example, you and I understand what is meant by the words "chocolate sundae." We understand what chocolate sundae means because someone taught us that was the name for the combination of certain sweet things. We also understand that the word "dessert" could also mean chocolate sundae or a number of equally appealing things to eat.

This is where we differ from our dogs. Pierre understands what "chicken" is because every time we say the word, he gets a piece of chicken. However, asking him if he wants "poultry" means nothing to him. Although Pierre may start salivating at the mere mention of the word "chicken," you could substitute the word "hammer" for "chicken," and as long as you use the word "hammer" every time you give Pierre a piece of chicken, it would soon mean the same thing.

Dogs can associate a word with a substance or an event (such as going outside or riding in a car), but using different words to express the same command, even if the words have the exact same meaning, will only confuse your dog. He simply can't make the connection. For example, automobile

Breed Truths

Female dogs do not read pregnancy books, nor do they ever attend a Lamaze class, yet they know everything there is to know with respect to the birth and care of their offspring. This is instinctual knowledge. Puppies nurse by instinct. Males are compelled to procreate through instinct. All dogs' behavior can be traced back to an instinct that once helped them survive.

and car have exactly the same meaning to you, but not to your dog. He can only associate a given word with one result.

Instinct

All dogs have some instinctive behaviors. This applies to the largest and the smallest of them. The reason for this is that all dogs, regardless of breed, descend from the same source—*Canis lupus*, the wolf.

That distant ancestor contributed certain genes to his descendants that have proven so necessary for a dog's existence that they are still in use. Granted, man has manipulated these hereditary inclinations to suit himself, but most of what dogs do can be traced back to the wolf.

From their lupine ancestor, dogs inherited a desire to chase. It's a good bet that even among the earliest wolves, some were more addicted to and adept at chasing than others, and so it has been with their descendants. We now have dogs that will chase a ball, a stick, or even the neighbor's cat only if they have nothing else to do. We also have dogs that will chase just about anything that moves—every time it moves! The chasers can be trained not to chase, but you will never be able to quell their *desire* to chase. The instinct courses heavily through their genetic makeup.

Some instinctive canine behaviors serve no real need for the domestic dog of today. Most dogs circle round and round on their bedding before lying down. It is believed that this behavior stems from the time when it was necessary to crush down the underbrush to make a comfortable bed for the night. Mother dogs regurgitate food for their puppies. This is carried over from the time when it was the most efficient way of bringing home the day's kill for their hungry pups.

No one teaches the modern dog any of these behaviors. These traits are contained within the genetic structure of each and every dog. Some of these traits are of little consequence today, but others conflict with how we want our dogs to behave as pets. The female's regurgitating her food even though we are feeding her puppies well or a male wandering away from home to locate the source of the scent he detects that tells him a female is in heat somewhere nearby can be a nuisance in modern life.

Rational Learning

As strong as the instinctual drive is, dogs can also think and make logical conclusions. When I drive down to the end of our country road and turn right to the highway, my dog sits calmly in his seat, gazes out the window, ready to go wherever his chauffeur may take him. However, if I turn left

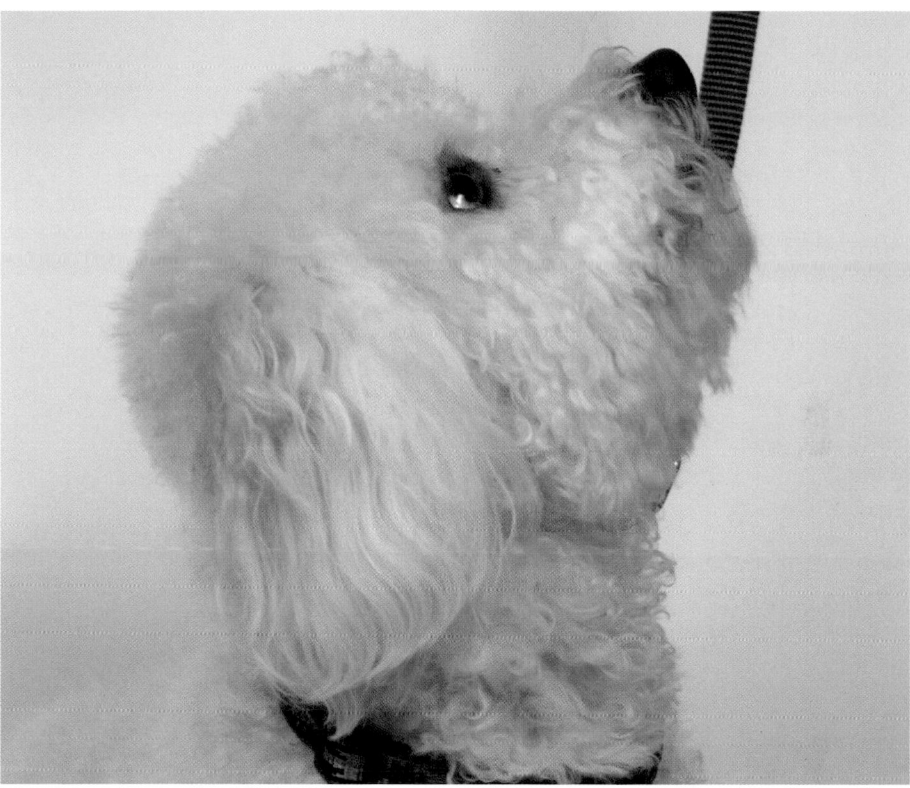

from our road, this means but one thing to him—we are on our way to the hiking trail! And then it's all I can do to keep him contained.

What causes a dog to rush out into the street and snatch a child from the danger of an oncoming auto? Who told our dogs that bringing us their leash or a toy will inspire a walk or playtime? There may be a scientific explanation for this behavior, but then I'm sure there are scientific explanations offered for almost everything, whether accurate or not.

Don't let a dog's ability to think rationally allow you to believe he will use good judgment. A dog is not going to let his good sense get in the way of instinctual behavior. Your dog won't stop and watch for cars when chasing his ball. His instinct will send him after the ball, traffic or not. Training is what will remind him that he has been taught to never run into the street for any reason.

How Training Works

A dog's concept of "good" and "bad" is not the same as a person's concept. For example, a dog has the natural need to eliminate. He doesn't care where he goes—it is his owner that cares. This is where you must reinforce his good behavior. If he relieves himself outside or in his designated area, he gets a treat. With enough positive reinforcement, he will soon know exactly what he is expected to do.

The only way your dog will learn to avoid breaking a specific rule is if there is a negative consequence every time he breaks or attempts to break that rule. Quite simply, he needs to learn that breaking rules equals unpleasant consequences and abiding by them results in reward of some kind. It is a formula easily understood by any dog. But in order for this to work, the unpleasant experience has to occur every single time the unwanted behavior occurs, and it must occur immediately upon breaking the law.

Being corrected for bad behavior some of the time or later in the day means absolutely nothing to a dog. Negative consequences then become something that happen at random, rather than as a result of having done something specific. Keep consistent and your dog will soon equate good behavior with positive rewards.

Why do dogs insist upon doing things that will get them in trouble? Your dog may know he will be in trouble when he raids the trashcan and scatters the contents over the kitchen floor, but the behavior continues.

This is about satisfying a need. There is no doubt that the dog got some reward—perhaps, the last of the prime rib—as a result of his first trash can raid. The next time it happened, the prize was a meaty soup bone. Now you have to think like a dog. Which is worse? Being reprimanded by you later or passing up the gourmet treat just a few nudges of the trash can away? After several successful trash can raids, your dog knows for certain there is a pot of gold under that lid. Forget the scolding! That comes later, the pork chop comes now.

PERSONALITY POINTERS

Active and Passive Behaviors

The canine world's body language is much simpler and far less ambiguous than the spoken one of humans. You can figure out a good part of a dog's body language very quickly by understanding two of a dog's attitudes: active and passive.

Active behavior:

1. Movement is in a forward and up direction.
2. Challenging dog steps forward, stiff-legged.
3. Often hair on the back of neck and shoulders is standing.
4. Head is up and he looks directly forward, staring at who or what is being challenged.
5. A snarl may emerge through clenched teeth.
6. Tail is stiffened and carried in a semi-erect position.
7. Stance and attitude indicate the dog's plans to move ahead with whatever action he needs to take.

Passive behavior:

1. Movement is in a backward and down direction folding up on himself.
2. Dog may roll over on back.
3. Head is lowered, ears are pinned back.
4. Tail is down and curled under body.

Whose fault is this? Yours! ("Of course," you think, "the parent always gets the blame!") But seriously, one of the most important principles of successful training has been ignored here—-avoidance. The trash should not have been made accessible to your dog in the first place. Now the problem behavior is set. And now that the dog has been able to raid the gourmet treasure box the second and third time, the thrill of victory was worth the agony of getting caught!

The more often your dog repeats an undesirable act, the more difficult it will be to remove that behavior from the dog's memory. It is being reinforced. That's why avoidance is a key part of your dog's training. If a dog never has a housebreaking accident indoors, you will not have to "untrain" that behavior before you begin to train the dog to go outdoors. If you do not allow your dog to chase the neighbor's cat, it will make it much easier on all of you (the neighbor, the cat, your dog, and you) than having to convince him that cat chasing is not fun.

There are transgressions that merit punishment, but the punishment itself must be appropriate. Having your brand-new rug chewed to bits or the stuffing pulled out of your sofa isn't exactly funny. However, don't make the

mistake of interpreting your dog's actions in human terms. What you may interpret as retaliation on the part of your dog is far more apt to be instinct, or even anxiety and frustration. Although it may appear your dog did something out of sheer spite, it is very important for you to understand this was not part of some diabolical plan to punish you.

I've had so many people tell me that their dog "pays them back" for being left behind by destroying the most expensive thing they can lay their teeth into. They have entirely misunderstood why their dog did what he did. First, dogs don't know what "expensive" or "valuable" means. Second, the dog simply missed his favorite person and got as close as he could to the loved one in the best way the dog knew how—locating and chewing on something his owner uses frequently. The owner of course has misinterpreted this behavior as retaliation.

Yelling and screaming will only make a bad situation worse, and a dog should never be hit or abused in any way. Because your tirade usually comes well after the fact, the dog is thoroughly confused by your behavior, and physical violence will not only endanger his welfare, but will make him mistrust and resent you. The only way to ensure that this kind of bad behavior will never happen again is to confine your dog to a safe place when you are away from him or if he is unsupervised. If you catch your dog in the act of doing something wrong, be calm, be fair, and be consistent. Don't punish a dog for something that he has been permitted to do before or do in another place.

This should give you some idea as to why a dog does or doesn't do what we think he should. Understanding how your dog works his way from A to Z will contribute tremendously to the success you will have in teaching him anything you want him to learn.

Trainability

Many dog trainers consider the more intelligent dog harder to train. Intelligence refers to a dog's ability to solve problems; trainability is the ease with which a dog can be convinced to take direction from a human. *Trainability is more important* to how people get along with their dogs than intelligence. Trainability is directly related to a dog's personality: his dependence and his willingness to do something for his owner or another human.

This is not a black and white situation, however. Few dogs are completely dependent or independent. Even if this were so, the highly-independent dog can be trained to respond with food and dogs with some aggressive tendencies can be motivated to forget about the initial inclination to bite. The Bichon Frise is a very trainable breed, making the trainer's work that much easier.

Breed Truths

The size of the Bichon Frise (especially the puppy) must be kept in mind throughout all training experiences. A hefty tug on the lead or a friendly thump on the rear of some of the larger breeds might well accomplish the trainer's goal, but the same kind of treatment can frighten the Bichon student and cause injury.

Shouting or screaming at a Bichon is more apt to make him want to escape than to respond. The breed is a gentle one and responds best to that kind of treatment.

Leash Training

It is never too early to accustom your puppy to a collar and leash. It is your way of keeping your dog under control. It may not be necessary for the puppy or adult dog to wear his collar and identification tags within the confines of your home, but no dog should ever leave home without a collar on and without the leash held securely in your hand.

Begin getting your dog or puppy accustomed to his collar by leaving it on for a few minutes at a time. Gradually extend the time you leave the collar on. Most dogs become accustomed to their collar very quickly and forget they are even wearing one.

Once this is accomplished, attach a lightweight leash to the collar while you are playing with the dog. Do not try to guide him at first. The point here is to accustom the pup to the feeling of having something attached to the collar.

Some puppies adapt to their collar very quickly and, without any undo resistance, learn to be guided with the leash. Other pups may be absolutely

adamant that they will not have any part of leash training and seem intent on strangling themselves before submitting.

If your puppy is one of the latter, do not continue to force the issue. Simply create a "lasso" with your leash and put your puppy's head and front legs through the lasso opening so that the leash encircles the puppy's shoulders and chest, just behind the front legs. Problem pups seem to object less to this method than to having the leash around their neck. Encourage your puppy to follow you as you move away. If the puppy is reluctant to cooperate, coax him along with a treat of some kind.

Hold the treat in front of the puppy's nose to encourage him to follow you. Just as soon as the puppy takes a few steps toward you, praise him enthusiastically and continue to do so as you move along.

Make the initial session very brief and enjoyable. Continue the lesson until the puppy is completely unconcerned about the fact that he is on a leash. With a treat in one hand and the leash in the other, you can begin to use both to guide the puppy in the direction you wish to go.

If your pup is the one that needed special treatment to get the leash lesson under way and is wearing the leash as a shoulder strap, wait until your walks are taken in stride before making any changes. You can then start attaching the leash to the puppy's collar, and chances are that there will no longer be any resistance.

Basic Commands

Helpful Hints

Once Pierre gets the routine under his belt use the *down* command for everything—earning his treats, for meals, going outdoors. Make *"Down"* a routine part of his life; he will soon view it as a fun trick rather than an action that indicates he is submitting to your will.

The *Down* Command

This can be a bit of a difficult one for both owner and dog because this is the command most apt to create those mixed messages we talked about earlier in this chapter. *"Down,"* from this point on can only mean one thing—*lie down*. Get off the sofa, and get off of me are *"Off."* Do not interchange these commands. If you do, you will confuse your dog and evoking the right response will become next to impossible.

The *down* command is difficult for your Bichon because it demands that he put himself into a submissive, vulnerable position. This is not the easiest thing for a dog to do on command. It's all a part of canine body language.

Because the *down* command has a negative association for your dog, you must do everything possible to associate it with as many positive rewards as you can. Food and high praise go a long way in this instance.

1. Have your dog assume the *sit* position. Kneel on his left side and hold a treat under his nose with your left hand. Slowly bring the treat down to the ground. He will follow the treat with his head and neck. As he does, say, *"Down"* and exert light pressure on his shoulders with your right hand. If he resists the pressure on his shoulders, do not continue pushing down. Doing so will only create more resistance.
2. An alternative method to get your dog headed into the down position is to draw his attention downward with the treat and slide your right hand under his front legs gently sliding them forward. As his forelegs begin to slide out to the front, keep moving the treat along the ground until his whole body is lying down while continuing to repeat, *"Down."*
3. Once Pierre has assumed the position you desire, give him the treat and praise him like he's just had some algorithmic breakthrough! Continue assisting him into the *down* position until he begins to do so on his own. Do not on any count get too demanding or harsh. The last thing you want to do is attach any more negative association to the command.

The *Come* Command

Learning to *come* teaches the dog that you are in command—the ultimate authority that must always be obeyed. Don't let your patience get in the way of teaching your dog that he must respond willingly and without fail. Pierre may decide that this is the lesson on which he is going to put his paw down and take your patience to the absolute limit. Dogs can be stubborn beyond imagination when it comes to *"Come."* After all, what's more fun, sniffing that intriguing scent left by some passing lady canine or giving up playtime to respond to your beck and call.

Of course, understanding why Pierre may not want to come does not alter the fact that he must. And there is the rub. Your temper flares and young Pierre begins to associate the *"Come"* word with the fact that you are angry and he is displeasing you.

No use trying to grit your teeth and pretend you aren't angry. Pierre will be able to see right through that. So, if you can't do this lesson for more than a minute or two without getting angry, you'll just have to limit yourself to that minute or two to begin with.

I recommend always using the command with the dog's name. Therefore, it is very important that even a very young puppy learn his name as soon as possible. Constant repetition of the dog's name usually does the trick. Use the puppy's name every time you speak to him. "Want to go outside, Pierre?" "Come, Pierre, come!"

It bears repeating that it is much easier to avoid the establishment of bad habits than it is to correct them once set. Do not give the *come* command unless you are certain your puppy will come to you. The very young puppy is far more inclined to respond to learning the *come* command than the older dog that is less dependent on you.

Initially, use the command when the puppy is already on his way to you or give the command while walking or running away from him. Clap your hands and sound very happy and excited about having the puppy join in on this "game." The very young dog will normally want to stay as close to his owner as possible, especially in strange surroundings. When your puppy sees you moving away, his natural inclination will be to get close to you. This is a perfect time to use the *come* command.

Later, as a puppy grows more self-confident and independent or if you are starting with an older puppy or an adult, it is best to attach a long leash or rope to the dog's collar to ensure the correct response. Again, no chasing, yelling, or punishing him for not obeying your command. It is imperative that you praise your puppy and give him a treat when he does come to you, even if he purposely delays responding for many minutes.

The *No* Command

One of the most important commands your puppy will ever learn is the meaning of the word *"No."* It is critical that the puppy learns this command just as soon as possible. Understanding that the command must be obeyed instantly could save your dog's life.

Running off and becoming lost, chasing a child or another animal into the road, or picking up and eating a harmful substance are not beyond the average dog's behavior. Your being able to stop the action instantly is obviously important in these situations and the word *"No"* is the shortest, quickest way to do so.

One important piece of advice in using this and all other commands—never give a command that you are not prepared and able to enforce. The only way a puppy learns to obey commands is to realize that once issued, commands must be complied with. Learning the *no* command should start on the first day of the puppy's arrival at your home.

The *Heel* Command

Having your dog *"Heel"* simply means that your dog will walk on your left side with his shoulder next to your leg on a loose leash. The dog will do this no matter which direction you might go or how quickly you turn. Teaching your dog to *heel* is really important because it will not only make your daily walks far more enjoyable, it will make for a far more tractable companion when the two of you are in crowded or confusing situations. I can't tell you how often I see people being pulled down the street in all but a flat-out horizontal position behind their dog. There is no reason for this to be going on, and mastering the *heel* command will help prevent this from happening.

You may want to begin the *heel* lesson a few steps at a time. Three or four steps at a time without pulling on the lead are three or four steps in the right direction. Take those pull-free steps, have your dog sit, and praise him to the high heavens. It is a good idea to change from the collar your dog normally wears to a special training collar constructed in a manner that will assist in the training. There are many different kinds of training collars that can be purchased, but bear in mind that these are meant for temporary use until your dog moves beyond his initial training, and they should never be left on your dog when he's alone.

Activities

The rewards of owning a Bichon are many but to gain access to what has earned Bichons their great reputation you must provide the framework from which your dog will reliably operate. These are things that every companion Bichon must be taught and must consider an ordinary everyday way of behaving. The American Kennel Club (AKC) and the United Kennel Club (UKC), the two registry systems here in the United States, have both acknowledged the benefits of obedience training by offering competitions in which your dog can earn obedience titles and championships. These events range from the somewhat informal Canine Good Citizen program to the complex and highly respected obedience degrees involving tracking and scent discrimination.

The Canine Good Citizen (CGC)

The Canine Good Citizen (CGC) program is aimed at making all dogs respected members of the community. Classes geared toward training the handler to qualify his dog are offered in most communities. Information on where these classes are conducted can be obtained from the place you shop for your dog's food and supplies, from local kennel clubs, or they may be listed in the classified section of your newspaper. The CGC is not a competition of any kind—the dog is scored only on his ability to master the basic requirements.

Therapy Work

Therapy dogs visit homes for the elderly, orphanages, and hospitals. Dogs with calm demeanors and good manners are best suited to make these visits and Bichons are naturals. Children and the elderly

BE PREPARED! The Canine Good Citizen Test

There are 10 parts to the Canine Good Citizen Test. Your dog must pass all ten in order to receive the CGC Certificate.

1. Appearance and grooming: The dog must be clean and appear to be free of parasites.
2. Acceptance of a friendly stranger: The dog is required to allow a friendly stranger to approach and speak to the handler.
3. Walking on a loose leash: The dog has to walk along attentively next to the handler.
4. Walking through a crowd: The dog is required to walk along, paying attention to the handler without interfering with other people or dogs.
5. *Sit* and *down* and *stay* on command: The dog must respond to each of the handler's commands.
6. *Come* when called: After being put in a *sit* or *lie down* position ten feet away, the dog must return to the handler when called.
7. *Sit* while touched by a stranger: A friendly stranger must be able to pet the dog.
8. Positive reaction to another dog: The dog has to keep his attention on the handler in the presence of another dog.
9. Calm reaction to distracting sights or noises: These distractions can be an unusual or loud noise or sight of a bicycle or unusual-looking object.
10. Supervised separation: The dog must wait calmly on leash while the owner is out of sight for three minutes.

Information regarding rules as well as when and where testing is held can be obtained directly from the American Kennel Club.

especially seem to light up when these dogs visit them, and it is amazing how sweet and gentle the therapy dogs can be.

Therapy work takes some training, because the dogs will be faced with situations they normally wouldn't be confronted with at home. The effort involved for dog and owner is more than rewarded in the sunshine it brings into peoples lives. Therapy Dogs International and the Delta Society can both provide additional information.

Tricks, Fun, and Games

Some people think that dogs don't have a sense of humor, but I disagree. I've had many that must have been standup comedians in another life. All did silly things that always elicited laughter from everyone in the family, and they did so with tails wagging and a sparkle in their eyes.

Other dogs I've owned approached life a bit more seriously, but that doesn't mean they were devoid of personality or that they didn't enjoy joining in on the fun. There are so many fun activities in which dogs are capable of participating with their owners, it would take an entire book just to list and explain them. Some owners find their Bichons are so good at certain games and activities that they set about pursuing slightly more formal outlets of exercise. Again, the sky's the limit. There are countless activities that provide the exercise that all dogs need, as well as limitless fun for both owner and dog.

Flyball

Flyball is undoubtedly one of the most exciting activities in which you and your dog can participate in. In this event, the dogs are organized into four teams. Each team races on a relay system. At the signal, each dog must clear four hurdles, release a ball from the flyball box, catch it in the air, and return with the ball to the starting point so that the next teammate can start. The team is racing against the clock, and the speed and excitement usually encourage the very enthusiastic ringside crowd.

Three titles can be earned: Flyball Dog (F.D.), Flyball Dog Excellent (F.D.X.), and Flyball Dog Champion (Fb.D.Ch.). Information regarding rules, training, and places where the events are held can be obtained directly from the North American Flyball Association, Inc.

Frisbee

Catching a Frisbee may not be every dog's "game du jour" but the dogs that love it, *love it!* Catching that plastic disc while it flies through the air becomes an obsession with some Bichons. For those addicted canines there are local, regional, and national Frisbee competitions. These competitions offer cash prizes ranging from hundreds to thousands of dollars. There are even international Frisbee teams that meet annually for the World Cup!

Leading pet shops usually carry information on these competitions. Both the Friskies Canine Frisbee Championships and the Alpo Frisbee Contest also provide information on their competitions.

Freestyle

Freestyle is something new for the canine athlete that might also be somewhat musically inclined. The sport combines obedience, dance, and calisthenics. Many of the basic obedience exercises are used, but in Freestyle, the movements are choreographed into a routine that is set to music. There are two main approaches to Freestyle: The Canine Freestyle Federation (CFF) emphasizes the dog's movements; the Musical Canine Sports International (MCSI) has a somewhat more colorful approach to the event, with consideration given to the handler's movements and costuming. Enthusiasm, the degree of difficulty in the movements displayed, and appropriateness of music and its interpretation are additional scoring factors. Detailed information can be obtained directly from the Canine Freestyle Federation

FYI: Earning Obedience Titles

Each level has a title that can be earned after attaining qualifying scores at a given number of shows.

Novice—earns a Companion Dog title (CD)

1. Heel on leash and figure eight.
2. Stand for examination.
3. Heel free.
4. Recall.
5. Long sit—one minute.
6. Long down—three minutes.

Open—earns Companion Dog Excellent title (CDX)

1. Heel off leash and figure eight.
2. Drop on recall.
3. Retrieve on flat.
4. Retrieve over high jump.
5. Broad jump.
6. Long sit—three minutes (with owner out of sight).
7. Long down—five minutes (with owner out of sight).

Utility—earns the Utility Dog title (UD)

1. Signal exercise.
2. Scent discrimination—Article 1.
3. Scent discrimination—Article 2.
4. Directed retrieve.
5. Moving stand and examination.
6. Directed jumping.

Those super dogs that have earned their Utility Dog titles are eligible to go on to compete for the next highest award—the Obedience Trial Championship (OTCh).

Standard Obedience

Obedience titles are earned when a dog performs a precise set of exercises. The exercises required in the various classes of competition range from Bichon basics like *heel*, *sit*, and *down* to Utility and Tracking Dog levels that require scent discrimination and directed jumping. The training and practice that dog and owner share in achieving these levels create a bond between the two that few other endeavors can equal.

Obedience Trial Championship (OTCh)

Tracking events have become very popular among dog owners, with many dogs now earning the rare Tracking Dog (TD) and Tracking Dog Excellent titles (TDX). A newer competition called Variable Surface Tracking (VST) is open to the dogs that have won their TD or TDX titles. When the competitors in this category have attained the qualifying scores they earn the VST designation.

Participating in organized events can be fun for both dog and owner. With a good training foundation, who knows how far your dog can go?

Rally

AKC Rally is a new dog sport that has been taking the nation by storm and is offered at shows and matches throughout the country. It is a successful stepping-stone from the AKC Canine Good Citizen program to the world of obedience or agility. Rally offers both the dogs and handlers an experience that is fun and energizing. The canine team moves at their own pace, very similar to rally-style auto racing. Rally was designed with the traditional pet owner in mind, but it can still be very challenging for those who enjoy higher levels of competition.

A rally course includes 10 to 20 stations, depending on the level. Scoring is not as rigorous as traditional obedience. Communication between handler and dog is encouraged and perfect *heel* position is not required, but there should be a sense of teamwork between the dog and handler. The main objective of rally is to produce dogs that have been trained to behave in the home, in public places, and in the presence of other dogs, in a manner that will reflect positively on the sport of rally at all times and under all conditions.

Agility

Agility competition is basically an obstacle course for dogs. Everyone involved, including the spectators, appears to be having the time of their lives, and the sport has become tremendously popular at dog shows and exhibitions from coast to coast. There are tunnels, catwalks, seesaws, and numerous other obstacles that the canine contestants have to master off leash, while being timed. It takes teamwork because the handler has to act as navigator.

Although the dogs do all the maneuvering, it is the handler who directs the dog, since the sequence of the individual obstacles is different at every event. Both the American Kennel Club and the U.S. Dog Agility Association can provide additional information, as well as names and addresses of the organizations sponsoring events nearest to your home.

Conformation Shows

The Bichon is a very popular show dog. Many owners who had thought of their Bichon only as a friend and companion have entered the dog show world and found it to be an exciting and fascinating hobby. The dog show fraternity extends around the entire world and affords competitors an opportunity to create new friendships from all walks of life. It is an activity in which one person, whether adult or child, or an entire family can participate.

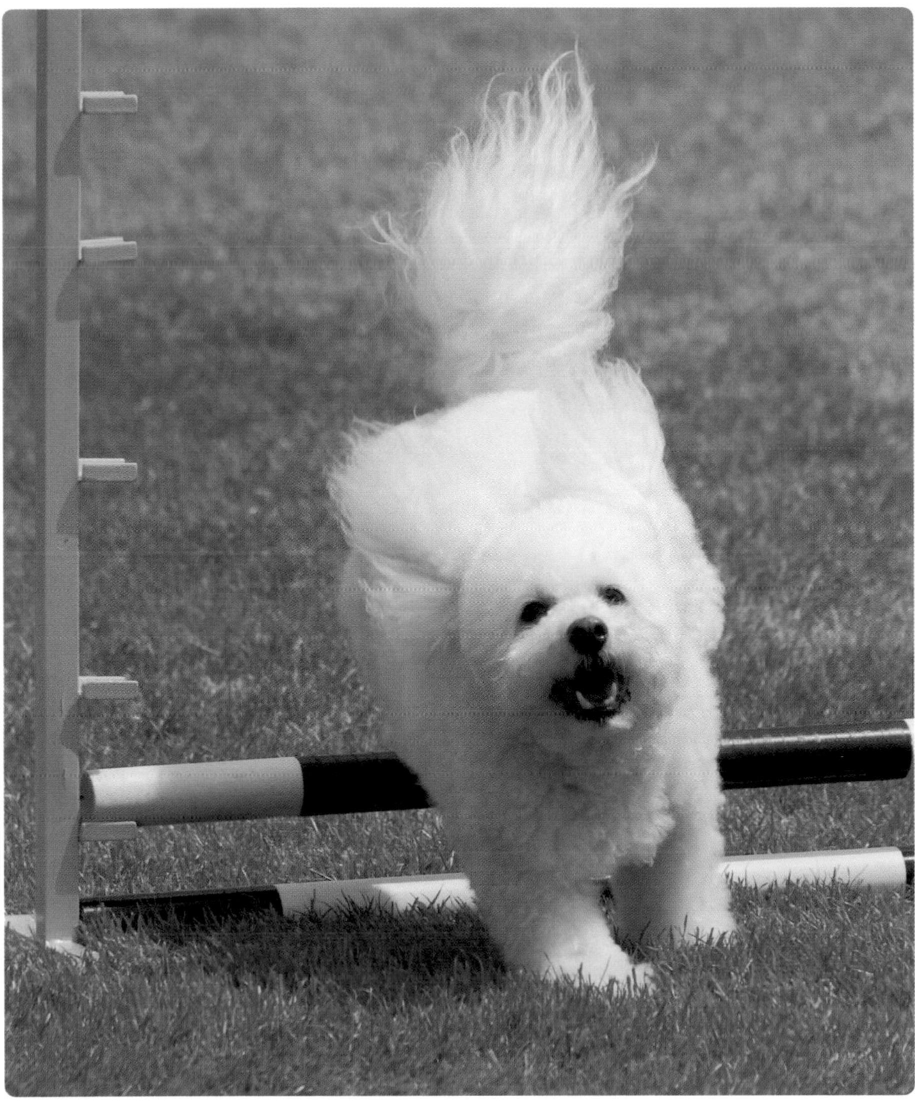

Conformation shows fall into two major categories: matches and championship events.

Match Shows

These are the less formal events that can be entered "on the day" and are offered to dogs as young as three months and older. They are a great place for beginners to learn to show their own dogs. They are totally relaxed and offer plenty of time for the novice handler to make mistakes along with everyone else and to ask questions and seek assistance from more experienced exhibitors.

Championship Shows

These are the more formal of the two events. The championship shows are sponsored by various all-breed kennel clubs or in some instances by a club specializing in one particular breed of dog. The American Kennel Club can provide you with the name of the all-breed kennel club in your area and the Bichon Frise Club of America can let you know if there is a local Bichon club.

AKC Championships are gained by accumulating points based on the number of entries in a dog's own breed and sex entered at the show. Of the fifteen points required, two of the wins must be what are called "majors" (i.e., three or more points). These two majors have to be won under two different judges.

All clubs sponsoring an American Kennel Club championship show must issue what is called a premium list. A premium list contains all the information you will need in order to enter that club's show. A professional show superintendent sends out these premium lists several weeks in advance of the closing date for entries for that show. A list of show superintendents can be obtained from the American Kennel Club. The entry form, which you will need to complete in order to enter the show, is included in the premium list.

The Road to Best in Show

Dog shows are a process of elimination, with one dog being named "Best in Show" at the end of the show. Only the Best of Breed winners advance to compete in the "Group" competitions. Each AKC-recognized breed falls into one of seven group classifications. The seven groups are Sporting, Hound, Working, Terrier, Toy, Non-Sporting and Herding. Four placements are awarded in each group, but only the first-place winner advances to the Best in Show competition.

Showing Your Bichon

Getting ready for a dog show begins long before you actually walk into the ring at a championship show. Beginners have a great deal to learn. It may seem totally overwhelming but keep in mind that everyone was a novice at one time. No matter how accomplished the pros around you may look, they did not know it all when they entered their first show.

Much of what you need to know is contained in books and magazine articles. Read everything that you can. Attend dog shows and observe the people in the ring who are winning

FYI: Classes of Competition

There are several classes in which you can enter your Bichon at American Kennel Club shows. Read the information contained in the premium list carefully. Often there are lower rates for puppy classes as well as other exceptions that you should be aware of.

Males and females compete separately within their respective breeds, in six regular classes. The following classes are offered, and are divided by sex.

Puppy For dogs between six and twelve months of age that are not yet a champion.

Twelve–Eighteen Months For dogs twelve to eighteen months of age that are not yet a champion.

Novice For dogs six months of age and over, which have not, prior to the date of closing of entries, won three first prizes in the Novice Class, a first prize in Bred-by-Exhibitor, American-bred, or Open Classes, nor one or more points toward their championship.

Bred by Exhibitor For dogs exhibited by their owner and breeder, but who are not yet a champion.

American-bred For dogs born in the United States from a mating that took place in the United States, that are not yet champions.

Open For any dog of the breed, at least six months of age.

After these classes are judged, all the dogs that won first place in a class compete again to see who is the best of the winning dogs. Males and females are judged separately. Only the best male (Winners Dog) and the best female (Winners Bitch) receive championship points. The Winners Dog and Winners Bitch then compete with the champions for the Best of Breed award. At the end of the Best of Breed Competition, three awards are given

Best of Breed The dog judged as the best in its breed category.

Best of Winners The dog judged as the better of the Winners Dog and Winners Bitch.

Best of Opposite Sex The best dog that is the opposite sex to the Best of Breed winner.

with their Bichons. You will quickly see how much skilled handling enhances a dog's looks and its chances of winning.

Junior Showmanship

The AKC offers youngsters 10 to 18 years of age the opportunity to compete with others their own age at various AKC events. Juniors competing in conformation events are judged on how they present their dogs. The AKC offers a booklet entitled "Regulations for Junior Showmanship" that can be obtained from that organization. The information the booklet contains can also be found on the AKC's web site.

Dog Show Judging Procedure

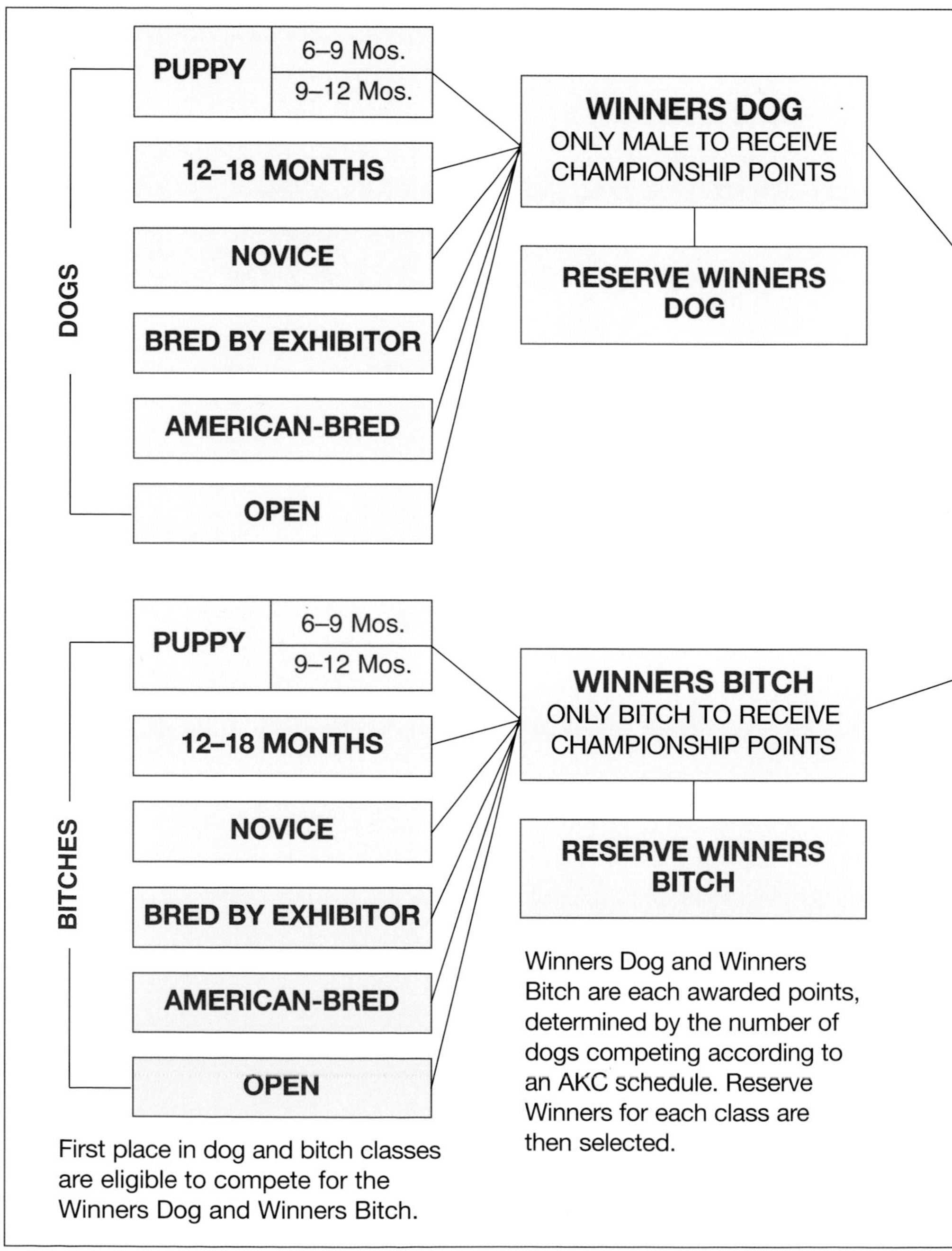

First place in dog and bitch classes are eligible to compete for the Winners Dog and Winners Bitch.

Winners Dog and Winners Bitch are each awarded points, determined by the number of dogs competing according to an AKC schedule. Reserve Winners for each class are then selected.

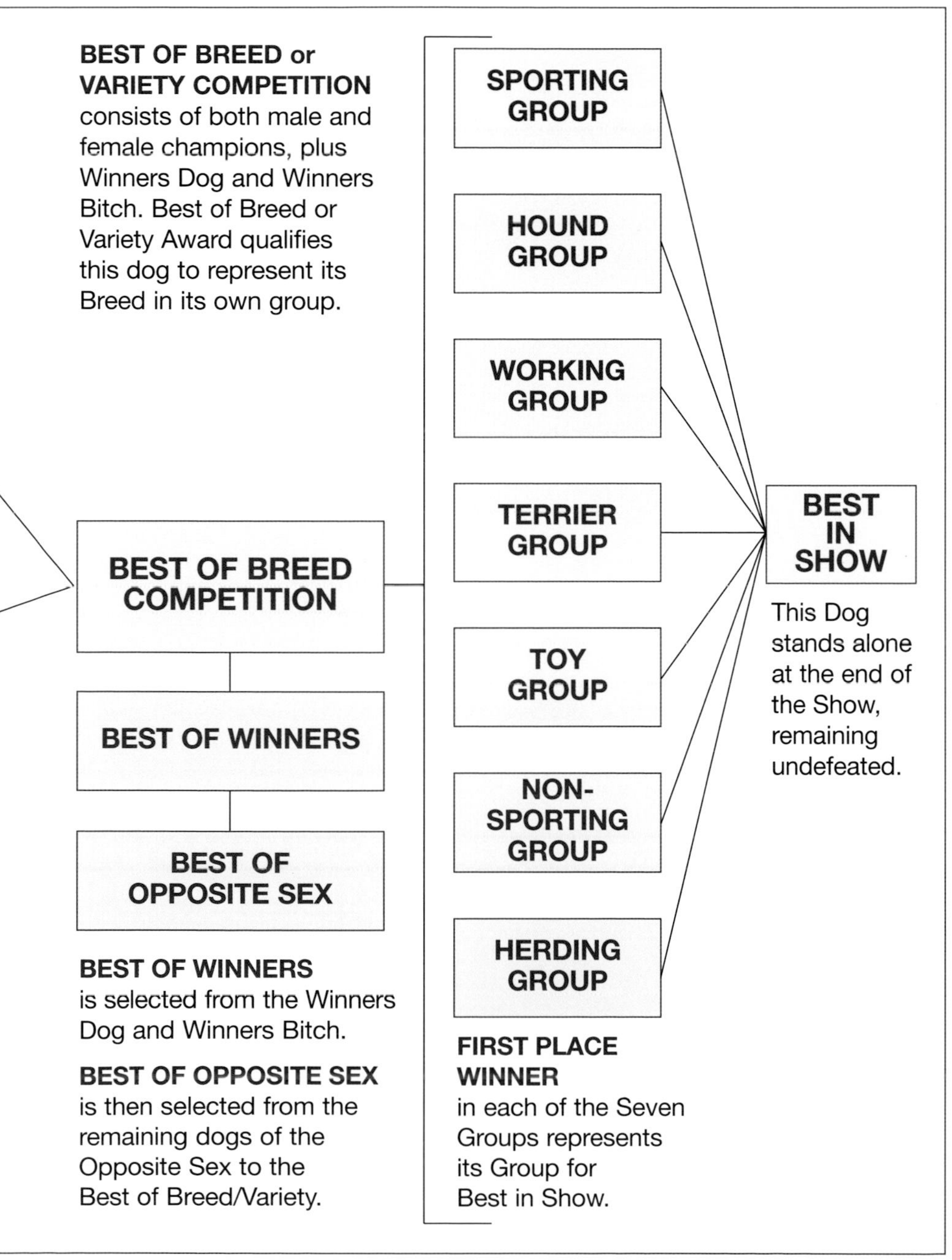
BEST OF BREED or VARIETY COMPETITION
consists of both male and female champions, plus Winners Dog and Winners Bitch. Best of Breed or Variety Award qualifies this dog to represent its Breed in its own group.
BEST OF BREED COMPETITION
BEST OF WINNERS
BEST OF OPPOSITE SEX
BEST OF WINNERS
is selected from the Winners Dog and Winners Bitch.
BEST OF OPPOSITE SEX
is then selected from the remaining dogs of the Opposite Sex to the Best of Breed/Variety.
SPORTING GROUP
HOUND GROUP
WORKING GROUP
TERRIER GROUP
TOY GROUP
NON-SPORTING GROUP
HERDING GROUP
FIRST PLACE WINNER
in each of the Seven Groups represents its Group for Best in Show.
BEST IN SHOW
This Dog stands alone at the end of the Show, remaining undefeated.

Leash Training

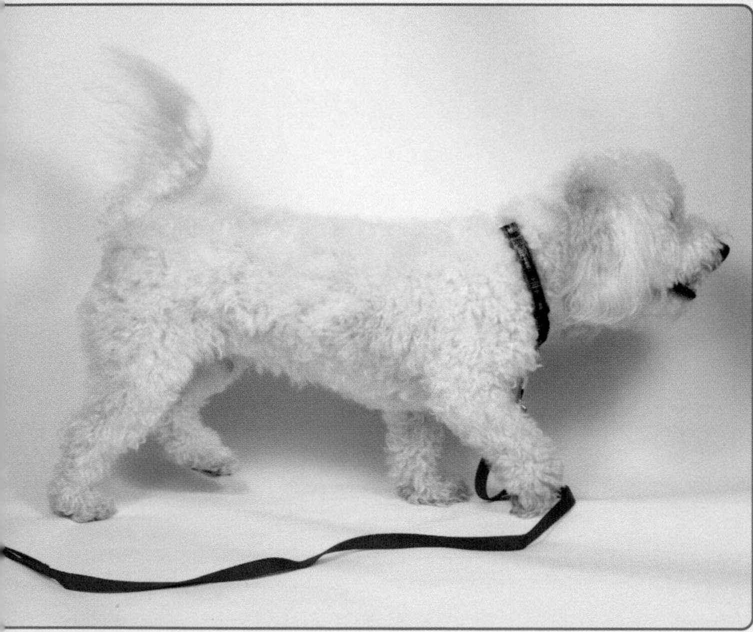

1 Place a soft collar around your puppy's neck. Although he will scratch a bit in no time at all he will forget it is even there.

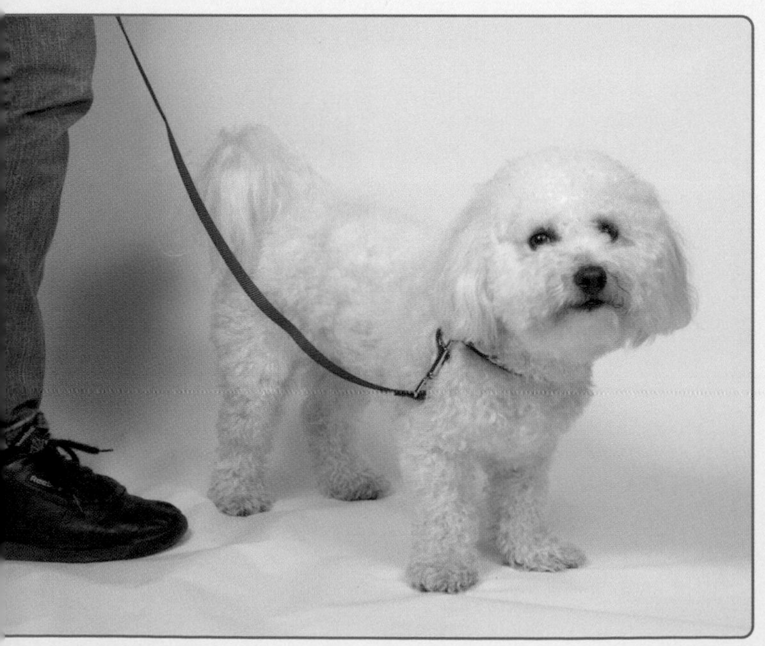

2 Attach a leash to the collar and let your puppy just pull it around for a few short periods.

3 Pick up the leash and follow your puppy around wherever he wants to go.

4 Hold a little treat in your fingers and begin to coax the puppy to follow you. Stay a few steps ahead of him and encourage him to come to you for the treat. Never pull or jerk on the leash. Within a day or two your puppy will begin to follow along with you. If he suddenly sits down or balks, use the treat to entice him along.

The *Sit* Command

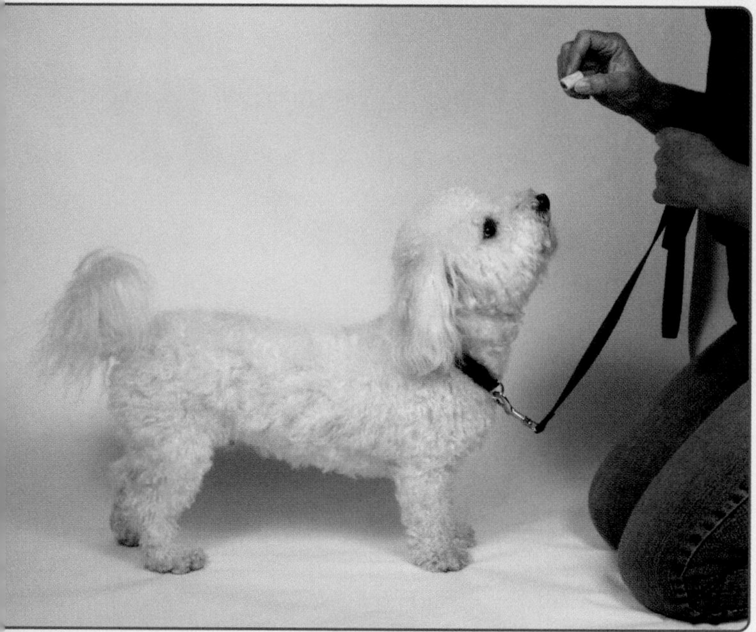

1 Your puppy should always be on collar and leash for her lessons. Young puppies are not beyond getting up and walking away when they have decided you and your lessons are boring.

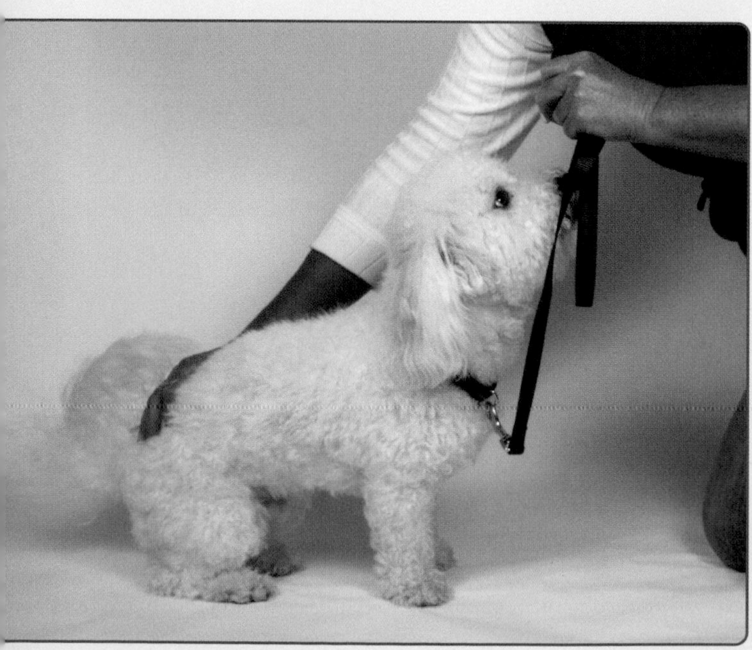

2 Kneel in front of your puppy and get his attention with a treat in your hand. Give the *"Pierre, sit"* command immediately before pushing down on his hindquarters or scooping his hind legs under him molding him into a *sit* position.

3 Praise him lavishly when he does *sit*, even though it is you who made it all happen. Again, a food treat always seems to get the lesson across to the learning youngster.

4 Continue holding your puppy's rear end down and repeat the *"Pierre, sit"* command several times. If your dog makes an attempt to get up, repeat the command yet again while exerting pressure on the rear end until the correct position is assumed.

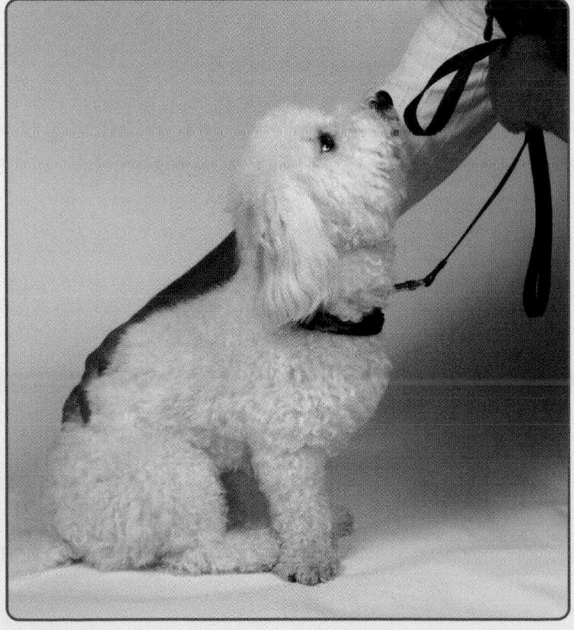

The *Stay* Command

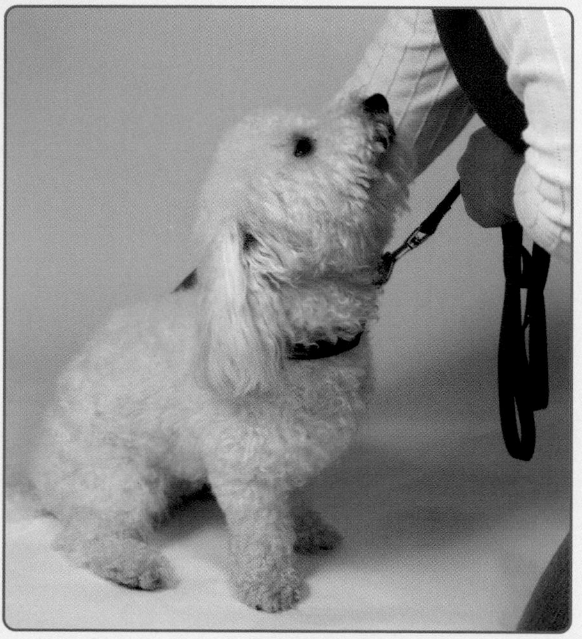

1 Make your Bichon stay in the *sit* position for increasing lengths of time. Begin with a few seconds and increase the time as lessons progress over the following weeks. Don't test a very young puppy's patience to the limits. As bright as the Bichon as a breed is, remember you are dealing with a baby. The attention span of any youngster, canine or human, is relatively short.

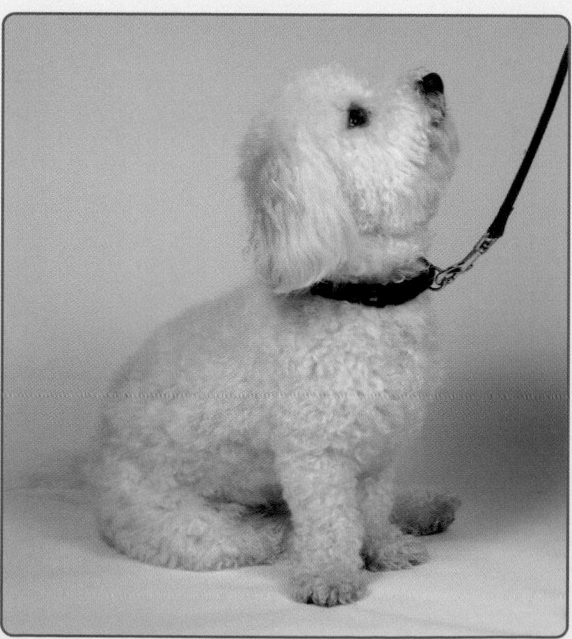

2 With Pierre on a leash and sitting in front of you, give him the "*Pierre, sit*" command.

3 Put the palm of your right hand in front of his eyes and say *"Pierre, stay!"* Take a small step back. If he attempts to get up and follow, step forward again and firmly say, *"Pierre, sit, stay!"* While you are saying this raise your hand, palm toward him, and again command *"Pierre, stay!"* Any attempt on his part to get up must be corrected at once, returning him to the *sit* position, holding your palm up and repeating, *"Pierre, stay!"*

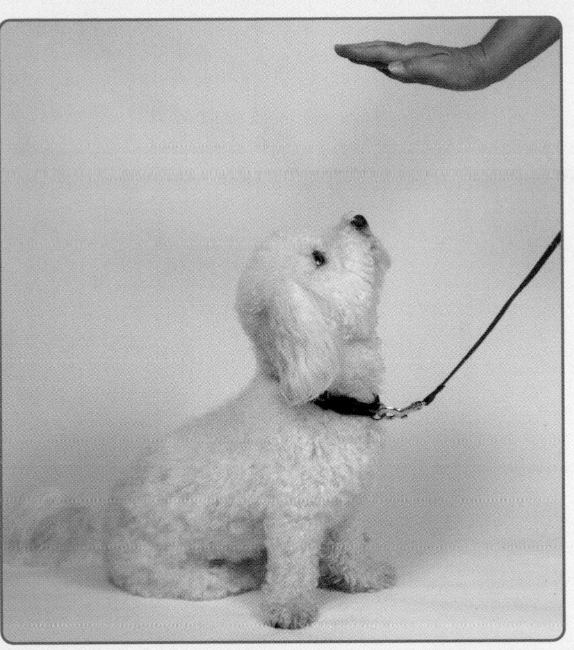

4 Once he begins to understand what you want, you can gradually increase the distance you step back. With a long leash attached to his collar (lightweight rope is fine) start with a few steps and gradually increase the distance to several yards.

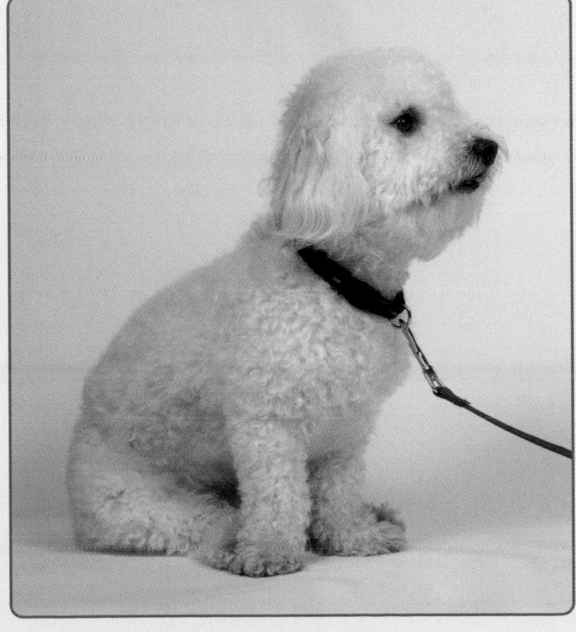

Chapter Eight

Grooming

What initially attracts most people to the Bichon Frise is his jaunty, sturdy look. His jet black eyes and nose are encircled by a halo of white that gives him a unique look among all breeds.

Shorn of his "crowning glory" the Bichon not only loses his distinction, but is robbed of that insulator that protects him from the cold of winter and heat of summer. There is an old wives tale that tells us long coated dogs should be shaved for the summer months to keep them cool. Nothing could be further from the truth.

The Bichon Frise is a double-coated breed. That is, he has a soft wooly undercoat and an outer coat consisting of harder hair. The combination of the two types of hair serves as an insulation against the elements—both hot and cold.

To preserve the look that attracted the new owner to the Bichon in the first place, he or she must be prepared to take care of that distinctive coat and keep it groomed not only to keep Pierre clean and healthy but also to maintain the wonderful look of the breed.

Breeders begin the grooming process while their puppies are still in the nest and by the time your little fellow is ready to join your household he has undoubtedly had to cope with regular home care—nail clipping, dental inspection, brushing, and clipping.

You must keep up this routine. If not you will find that it will take some retraining to teach your Bichon that this is a part of his day-to-day existence. You and your new addition are going to spend a considerable amount of time together accomplishing those grooming chores so I suggest you make the time as enjoyable and easy as possible for the both of you.

The very young Bichon puppy doesn't require a whole lot of grooming. A good brush and comb can take care of the majority of it. However, you will find that tiny Pierre will grow like a weed in the early months of his life and along with that growth will come more time required to keep his coat properly cared for.

Some new owners choose to learn to groom and clip their Bichons themselves. Others leave the major work to the professional groomer and just do

the maintenance work between regular appointments. Regardless, there are certain basic grooming tools you will need to start off with. You will need a good brush and comb from the first day your puppy arrives until he is a senior citizen.

CAUTION

Even if you plan to handle all of your Bichon's grooming chores yourself I highly recommend a few trips to the professional groomer while your puppy is still young. Not only will it help establish a grooming "pattern" to follow, it will also accustom your youngster to the hustle and bustle of the grooming shop and being groomed by strangers. Inevitably, there will come a time when you can't attend to your Bichon's grooming chores or when you want him to look especially good for a special occasion. If you wait until he is an adult for his first experience at the grooming parlor, he could easily be terrorized by something so strange and new.

The best brush for puppy hair is called a "slicker brush." It is an oblong metal brush with curved pins set in rubber. This brush can be used all over the young Bichon and on the shorter hair and legs of the adult Bichon. Care must be taken in using this brush in that it can scratch the skin of your puppy if not used gently and it can pull out the undercoat of the adult Bichon if not used correctly.

The most useful comb for the Bichon is what groomers refer to as a "Greyhound comb." This is a metal comb about 8 inches long divided in half with teeth set very close on one half and wider on the other half. This comb helps with mats, tangles, and also to make the hair stand out from the body to achieve that "teddy bear" look.

CHECKLIST

Grooming Equipment

In order for the amateur groomer to learn how to accomplish the finished look that professionals are able to create there are a number of bottom line items of equipment that are necessary. Most of this equipment can be obtained at your local pet emporium or beauty supply shops for humans. This is all equipment that you will be able to use for the life of your Bichon so when prorated over the length of time you will use it even the best possible quality represents a miniscule investment.

- ✔ **Grooming table** Major considerations are size that is correct for the adult Bichon and height that allows you to work comfortably in a standing position.
- ✔ **Pin brush** Also referred to as a "Poodle brush" this sports long pliable metal bristles set in rubber. This brush is necessary for the adult Bichon's longer hair and for brush drying the coat after a bath.
- ✔ **Slicker brush** This multipurpose brush will prove useful from puppyhood on.
- ✔ **Greyhound comb** Slip this into your back pocket or backpack for quick touchups and to help remove tangles and debris while out on a hike.
- ✔ **Tweezers or hemostat** Either can be used to remove the hair that grows inside a Bichon's ears and causes wax to accumulate.
- ✔ **Shampoo** Choose one especially formulated for white dog hair
- ✔ **Baby or grooming powder** This is very useful in helping to separate mats and tangles.
- ✔ **Electric hair clippers, scissors, curved scissors** These items will become more and more useful as your Bichon matures and especially if you plan to keep him in trim yourself. High-quality products are well worth the investment and will last a lifetime.

Grooming is a part of your Bichon's life so make it as easy to accomplish as possible. Don't attempt to do it sitting on the floor (you'll spend most of your time trying to keep the little fellow in place) or with the Bichon sitting on your lap. Buy or build yourself a good grooming table. A card table equipped with a nonskid pad can be used if it is of the correct height for you to work in a standing position. The problem with a card table is that the large area makes most dogs want to move away from the groomer.

A grooming table of the proper size—just large enough for the adult Bichon to stand and lie down on—will ease your task considerably especially if it is of the height that allows you to work comfortably. Several owners I know adjust their grooming tables to a height that can accommodate being used while they are sitting and watching television. Adjustable grooming tables can be purchased at most of the major pet chains and will prove their worth as your Bichon's coat matures.

Some owners have found that they enjoy the look of the full-coated mature Bichon and are willing to invest the time involved in keeping the hair well groomed.

Another important lesson your Bichon must learn is lie on his side while you brush. Teaching him to do so will save you all kinds of time and allow you to easily reach those hard to get to places, such as under his "arms" and around the genitalia.

The easiest way to train your Bichon to do this is to pick him up from the grooming table while he is in a standing position. Put your hands around his front and rear and hold him to your chest. Lean forward and lay him down on his side on the grooming table. Comfort him and say, *"Stay."* Encourage him to stay in that position by holding your hands palms down on his side and repeating *"Stay"* and "Good boy." It will take a bit of time for Pierre to relax in this position but eventually he will become totally cooperative. Many Bichons will be found to doze off and take a trip to dreamland during their grooming sessions.

Helpful Hints

At around 10 months of age you will note that your Bichon puppy's coat will begin to change. Coarser guard hairs appear at the top of the shoulders and on the back toward the tail. These changes represent the early stages of adult coat development. It will take up to a full year for the coat to fully mature but it is important to keep up with regular grooming sessions because this is the coat stage when mats are not uncommon. The Bichon's adult hair is not only of an entirely different texture; it grows much longer and much thicker.

The pin brush with its longer bristles set in rubber is far more effective for line-brushing the adult Bichon coat and is also less apt to tear out the longer hair.

Line Brushing

If you begin this technique when Pierre is still a puppy he will be completely accustomed to the process long before his adult, more time-consuming coat has developed, which is when proper grooming is extremely important. With your Bichon lying on his side, begin at the side front and make a part in the hair. Thoroughly brush that line from the skin out and then make another part a bit further down repeating the brushing process. Continue this through to the rear of the puppy. Brush through the hair to the right and left of the part. Do a small section at a time. *Part and brush.* You will repeat this process working toward the rear until you reach your puppy's tail.

Do the legs on the same side. Use the same process, parting the hair at the top of the leg and working down. Do this all around the leg. Be especially careful to attend to the hard-to-reach areas under the upper legs where they join the body and along the neck under the ears as mats occur in these areas quickly.

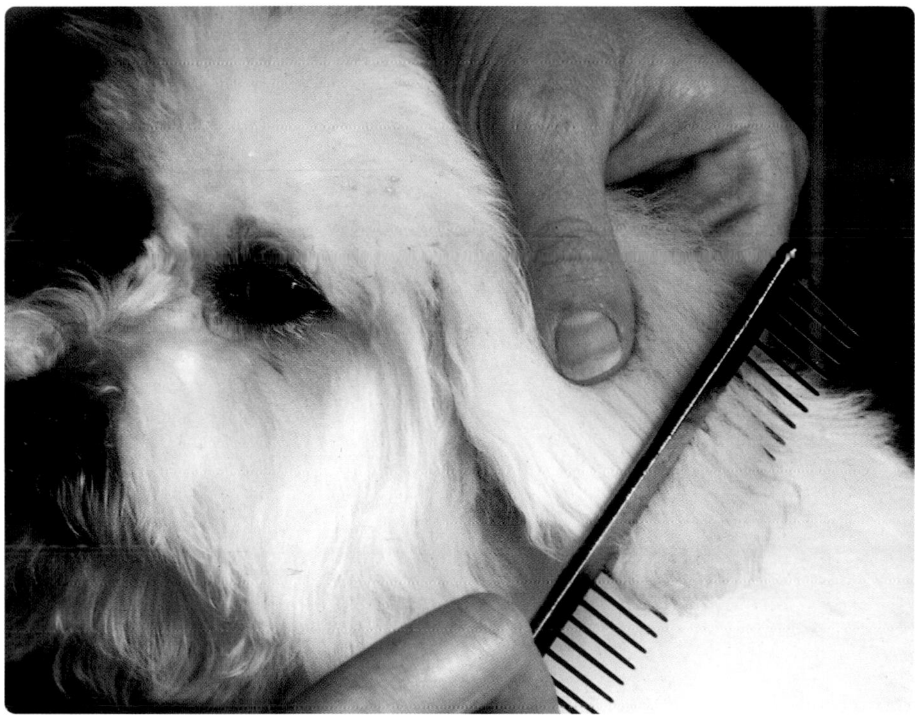

Some mats refuse to be brushed out easily. If this is the case, use your fingers and the Greyhound comb to separate the hairs out as much as you possibly can. Cutting the mat out will leave a big hole in his coat that will take a considerable length of time to grow back in. Apply baby powder or one of the especially prepared grooming powders directly to the mat. Then brush completely from the skin out. You will lose a bit of hair in the process but considerably less than cutting or pulling would cause.

With your puppy standing, you can start with the head, chest, and tail areas. When brushing the longer hair of the tail and face, do so gently so as not to break the hair. When brushing on and around the rear legs make sure to give special care and attention to the area of the anus and genitalia.

Nail Trimming

A regular part of your grooming routine should be devoted to inspecting your Bichon's feet and trimming back his nails. Always inspect his feet for cracked pads and check between the toes for splinters and thorns. Pay particular attention to any swollen or tender areas.

The nails of the Bichon who spends most of his time indoors or on grass when outdoors can grow long very quickly. Do not allow your dog's nails to become overgrown and then expect to cut them back easily.

Many pet owners are extremely reluctant to attempt trimming their dogs' nails. It is important not to allow your Bichon to convince you that nail trimming is traumatic or painful. Bichons can be extremely convincing actors. Allowing your Bichon to set down the rules for grooming would be the same as permitting children to decide when they should bathe or brush their teeth.

Bi-weekly nail care is important and will take so little time that your Bichon will soon become totally accustomed to having it done. It is, however, important to know that each nail has a blood vessel running through the center called the "quick." The quick grows close to the end of the nail and contains very sensitive nerve endings. The point is to have a minimum amount of nail to surround the quick.

If the nail is allowed to grow too long it will be impossible to cut it back to a proper length without cutting into the quick. This causes severe pain to the dog and can also result in a great deal of bleeding that can be difficult to stop. Taking small nips off the nails rather than one large chunk will guard against cutting into the quick.

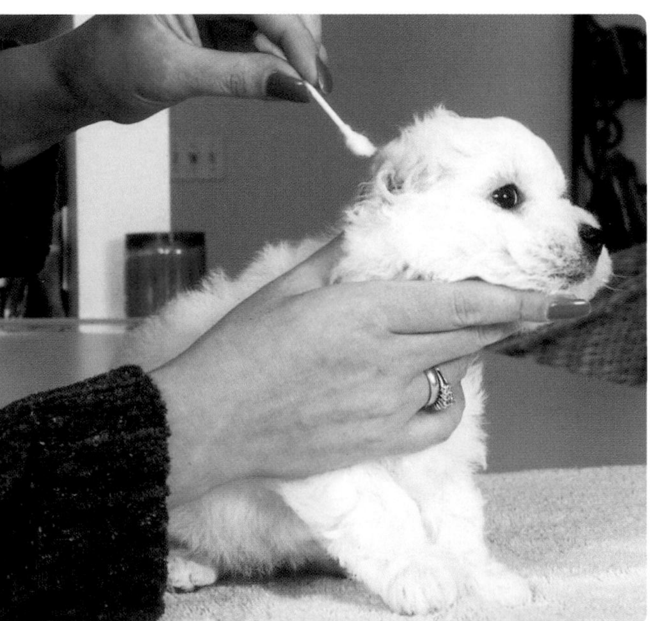

Should you nip the quick and bleeding occur, there are a number of blood clotting products available at pet shops that will almost immediately stem the flow. It is wise to have one of these products on hand in case there is a nail trimming accident or your Bichon tears his own nail.

Ear Care

Check the inside of the ear for accumulated wax and dirt. Begin by removing the long hair that leads to the ear canal. Use tweezers or a hemostat to pull out the excess hair. If this area is blocked, serious ear problems can occur. After removing the hair, dampen a Q-Tip with alcohol and carefully clean out the canal. Apply a bacterium inhibiting powder made for the purpose and available at most pet supply stores. Never probe into the ear canal with anything smaller than your fingertip. If wax seems to build up often or if you notice any strong odor when you lift the ear, have your vet check for a possible ear infection. Other indications of ear problems are constant shaking the head, scratching, or holding the head tilted to one side.

Hair should be removed from the ear canal before bathing. Cleaning the ears is a vitally important part of Bichon grooming. If done periodically your dog's ears will stay clean and the process will only take a few minutes.

Dental Hygiene

In the wild, animals keep their teeth clean by chewing through tough bone, muscle, and hide to get the food they need to sustain themselves. Humans serve their dogs prepared foods that only require swallowing. Thus, teeth become neglected and decay sets in. Some Bichons love to chew hard dog biscuits and this keeps their teeth relatively clean. But not all dogs chew enough to keep their teeth in good order.

If your dog isn't doing the job himself, you will have to help the situation along by brushing his teeth. Most dogs learn to submit to having their teeth brushed very quickly. Brush your Bichon's teeth at least once a week with toothpaste designed for dogs. Do not use toothpaste developed for human use as most contain sugar that will only add to your dog's problems. If plaque buildup has occurred, make an appointment to have it removed by your veterinarian.

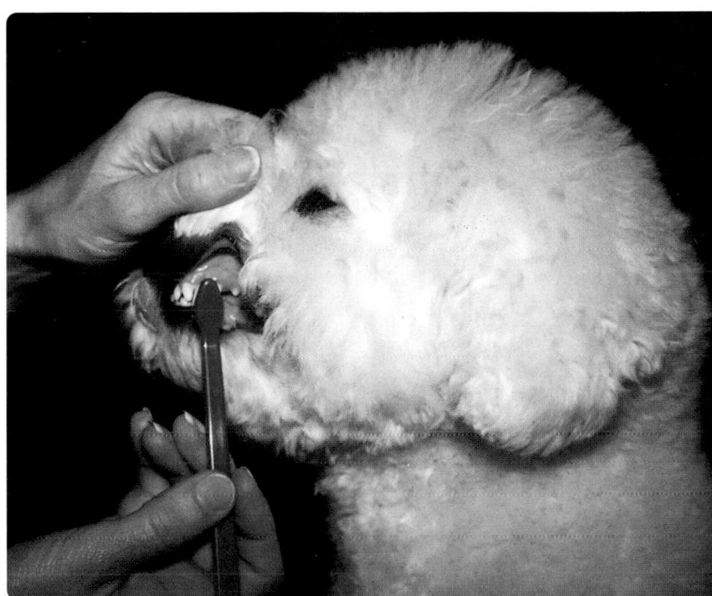

Anal Glands

The anal glands are located on each side of the anus. They collect a foul-smelling fluid that the dog may release when he gets excited or fearful or when he's marking his territory. Normally, the fluid is released whenever your dog has a bowel movement. If the drainage of the glands becomes obstructed, your dog may experience discomfort, such as an itching feeling. You may notice your dog sitting on his rear, dragging his bottom by his front feet, or biting his tail area.

Relieving the blockage is an unpleasant task, but experienced dog owners can do it at home. However, most owners turn to groomer or veterinary personnel for help, because pet-care professionals know exactly how to express the liquid quickly and easily. If your dog acts like he is in pain when you touch the anal area, you will need to see your veterinarian. Infections of the glands require antibiotics for treatment, and in some cases, surgical removal is required.

If you wish to accomplish this task yourself, do so at bath time. With the dog in the tub, place your thumb and forefinger on either side of the anal passage and exert pressure. The glands will quickly empty.

Bathing

The Bichon's coat must be completely brushed out and mat free before you even think about bathing. Water added to a matted coat will "felt," creating a solid lump of hair that cannot be disentangled or brushed out.

Once your Bichon is thoroughly brushed out, get everything ready that you will need. Not all dogs love bath time and the last thing you'll want to have happen is Pierre deciding he is going to leap out of the tub while you are hunting for the shampoo or a washcloth.

Before you begin to wet the coat, place cotton balls inside your dog's ears to avoid water running down into the ear canal. Then put a tiny dab of mineral oil or petroleum jelly into each eye to protect the eye from the shampoo.

Ideally, the basin in which you bathe your dog will be at a height that is comfortable for you to work in a standing position. Having to bend down and over a ground-level bathtub is not easy and will make you rush through the bathing/rinsing process, which can lead to skin problems.

Using the rubber spray hose, thoroughly soak your Bichon's coat. The spray hose is an absolutely necessary tool for the rinsing process as well. It is the only way you can be sure that all shampoo residue is removed from the coat.

Once the coat is thoroughly wet, apply the shampoo on the neck directly behind the ears. Work shampoo into the coat all around the neck. Add additional shampoo in a line down the back and work into the coat all around the body and down the legs and tail.

Work the shampoo well down to the skin. Allow the suds to remain in the coat while you attend to the head. This will assist the whitening process. Use a washcloth to lather the head and face, being careful that the suds don't get into your dog's eyes, nose, and mouth.

Use the washcloth to rinse the shampoo off the head. You can use the spray hose to assist you in doing this but if you do, turn the water pressure

CHECKLIST

Standby Bath Time Essentials

- ✔ Nonskid rubber mat for bottom of tub or washbasin
- ✔ Rubber spray hose
- ✔ Cotton balls for inside your Bichon's ears
- ✔ Shampoo formulated especially for white dogs
- ✔ Mineral oil or petroleum jelly to protect the eye from shampoo irritation.
- ✔ Heavy towels
- ✔ Pin brush and electric dryer for brush drying
- ✔ Washcloth

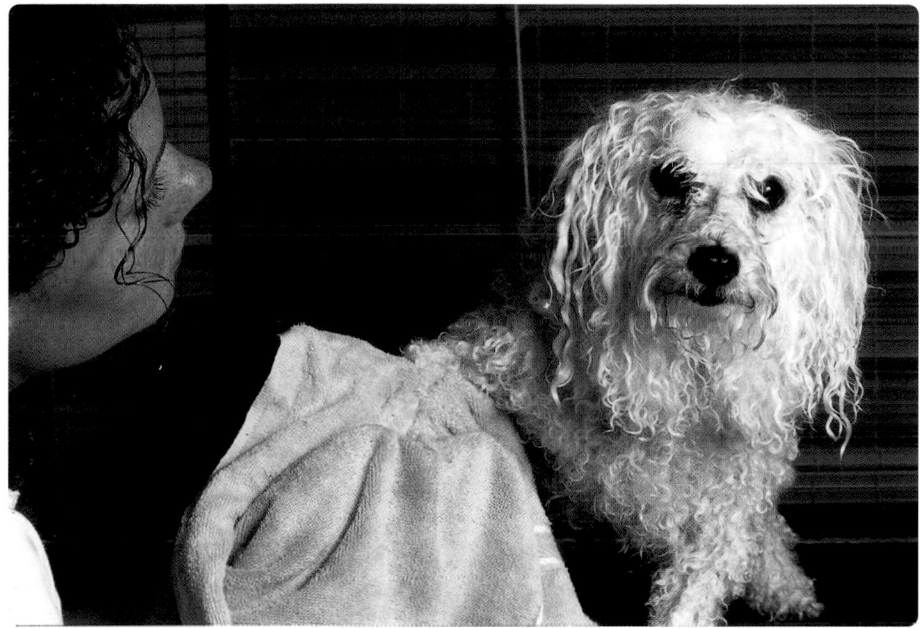

down and allow the water to very gently rinse the soap away. You can then turn the pressure back up a bit to rinse back from the head. Rinse the coat thoroughly at least twice. Allowing shampoo residue to remain in the coat is sure to create dry skin that will make your Bichon scratch.

Once you are certain that you have rinsed away the entire shampoo residue squeeze as much of the water out of the coat as possible. Wrap your Bichon in one of the heavy towels and carry him to the grooming table. Remove the cotton from his ears and pat dry with the towel. Use another towel if the coat still appears too wet. You are not trying to dry the coat, only remove all the excess water.

Brush Drying

All it takes to dry a smooth coated dog is a couple of big towels. Drying a Bichon is a much more elaborate process and one that is important if you want Pierre to maintain that fluffy teddy bear look.

It is very important to "brush dry" your Bichon using your pin brush (or slicker if the hair is short) and a hair dryer if you also plan on trimming him yourself. If you allow a Bichon's hair to dry without brushing, the hair will curl and it will be completely impossible to scissors the coat properly.

If you do plan on learning to trim yourself I strongly suggest that you invest in a hair dryer that has its own stand. It will simplify the task by allowing you to use both your hands to do the brushing and the more powerful dryer will reduce the time it takes to dry a Bichon by half.

Right after a quick towel drying, use your pin brush to go through the damp coat to remove any tangles. Set your hair dryer at "medium." Never use the "hot" setting in an attempt to finish the job more quickly. It may be quicker but that setting will also dry out the hair and could easily burn the skin of your Bichon.

With Pierre lying on his side use the line brushing method with your pin brush. Point the dryer at the area to be brushed, using light strokes repeatedly until that section is completely dry, and then move on to the next section. Brush gently and be careful not to pull hair out. Once the body is dry, brush out the head, legs, and tail.

Just as soon as your Bichon is completely dry, begin the trimming process. Waiting too long after brush drying will give the coat time to start curling and make getting a nice smooth finish to your trim job almost impossible. All your brush-drying efforts will be wasted.

What's in a Trim?

If the purpose in getting Pierre groomed and trimmed is so that you can appreciate his good looks, you can learn to do this yourself. However, if grooming is being done for the show ring, a professional's touch is needed. Preparing a Bichon Frise for the show ring is an art that is perfected after many years of trial and error. If you expect Pierre to bring home those blue ribbons, have an experienced show ring groomer do the job.

Scissoring

"Practice makes perfect." That old adage certainly applies to learning how to scissors your Bichon. Study the photos that appear throughout this book and do your utmost to create a similar picture out of the woolly mass that stands before you on your grooming table.

While trimming, remember to continually lift the hair up and away from the body with your comb as you go along. This keeps the entire coat standing up and with practice you will be able to achieve the smooth but plush look you are after.

The hair of the Bichon's beard, ears, and tail is always kept much longer than the rest of the coat. The actual length depends upon what you find easiest to maintain but remember that you are attempting to trim in the look of the breed.

The object in trimming the Bichon's head is to create a continuous rounded look that encompasses the ears and beard. There is no indentation where the ears join the head. The complete circular look is one of the things that differentiate the Bichon's look from that of the Poodle.

To have the ears lie into the circle you are attempting to create you may have to trim away a little of the hair along the neck under the ear. Remember, when cutting hair—*a little at a time.* You can always take more off to achieve the look you are after but you can't put hair back if you've taken off too much.

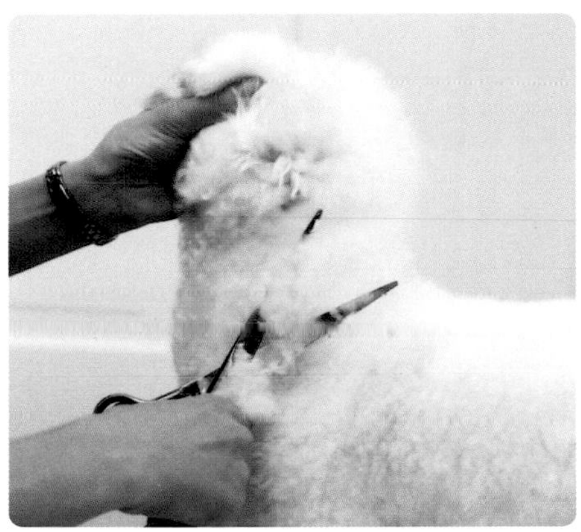

In order not to have the ear stand too far away from the head you must remove some of the hair along the neck under the ear. Facing your Bichon head on, your goal is to create a straight line from the outside of the ear on down to the foot. Begin the side trim under the ear and work down. Continue scissoring on down the shoulder.

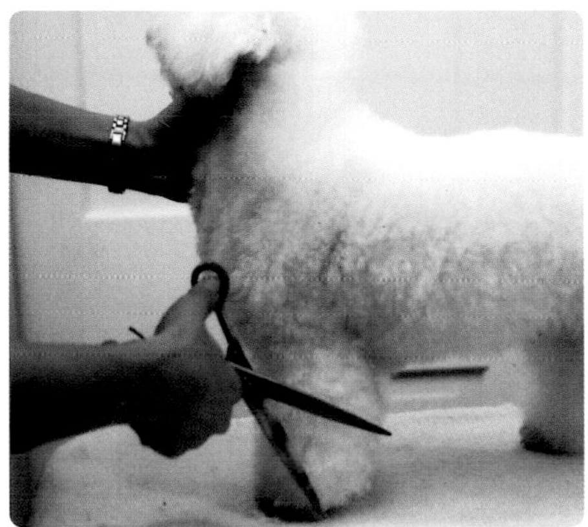

When you reach the foot, scissor around the leg to create a cylinder. Use the hair length on the outside of the leg as a guide for length around the entire leg. Once completed go to the other side of the dog and complete the under-ear-to-foot scissoring and rounding of the leg. If you have electric clippers, you can touch up that under-ear-to-foot line to make it straighter.

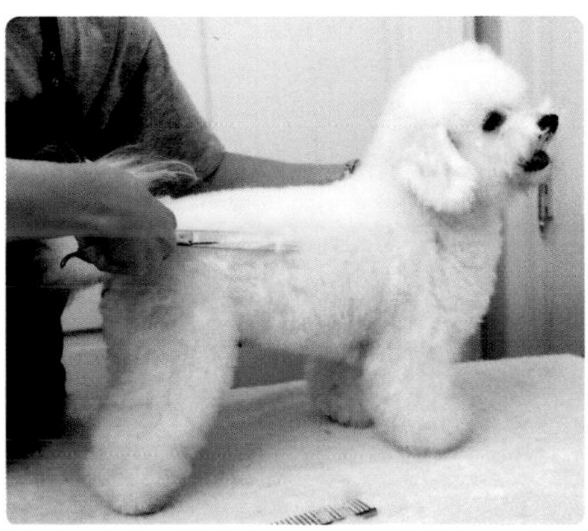

Next step is to trim the sides of your Bichon using the shoulder length hair as a guide to length for the body. Continue right on to the root of the tail and down to the hip. Continue down the thigh and rear leg to the foot. Repeat that process on the other side of the dog. Round off the rear legs as you did the front legs.

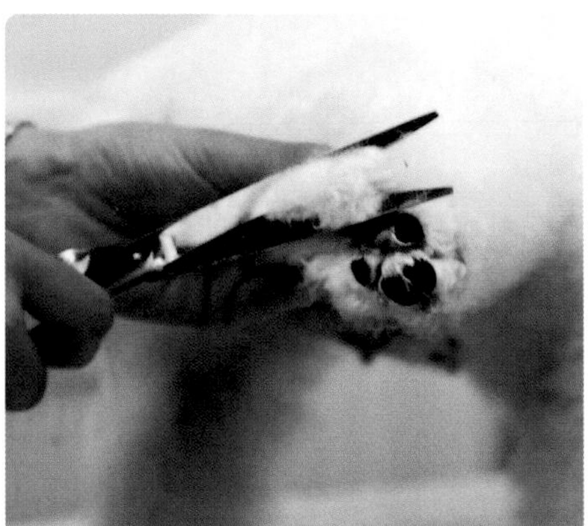

Lift the front foot up and scissor to round the bottom outside edges to match the cylinder effect of the leg. Repeat on the other foot. Repeat the rounding process on the rear feet. With electric clippers or scissors trim out the hair that grows between the pads of the feet.

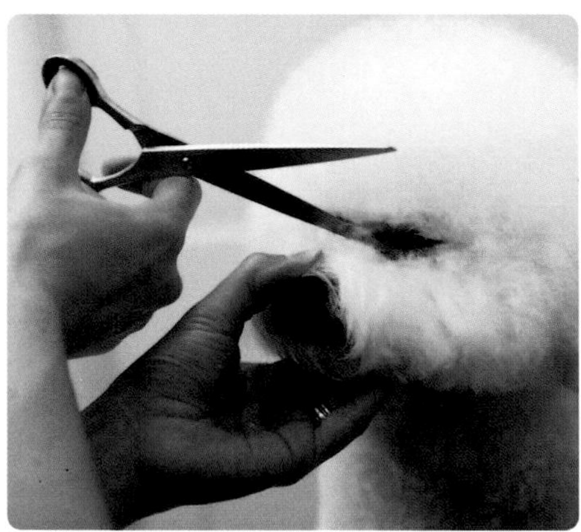

Head trim: Comb the hair of your Bichon's forehead forward toward the nose. Using the straight scissors, cut a straight line parallel to the forehead so that the eyes are revealed.

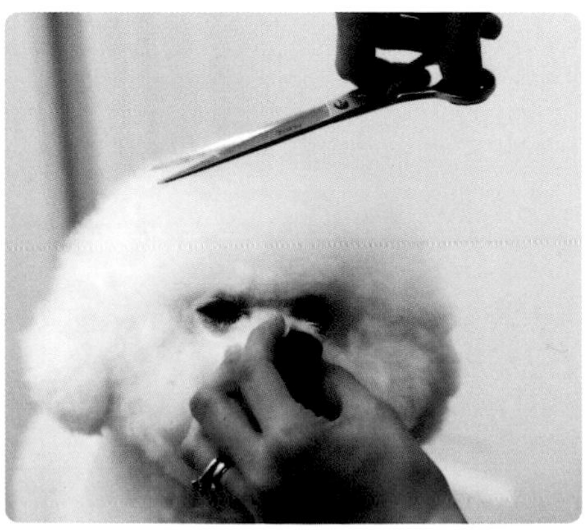

Step to the side of the head and using your curved sheers cut the head hair in a circular fashion from just above the eyes to the back of the skull.

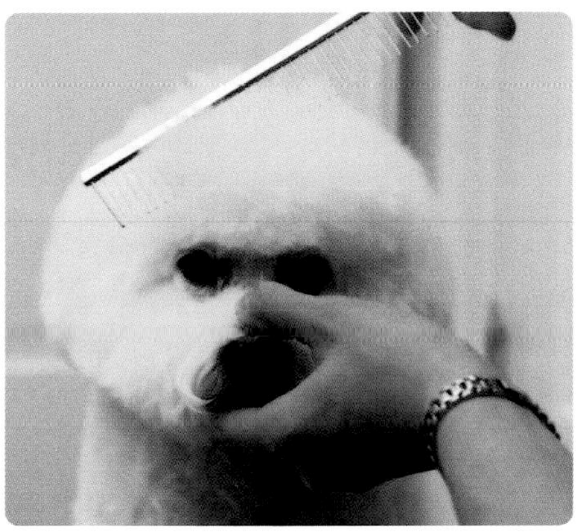

Return to the front of the head; comb the hair up and out and trim to smooth out the circular look viewed from the front and from the sides.

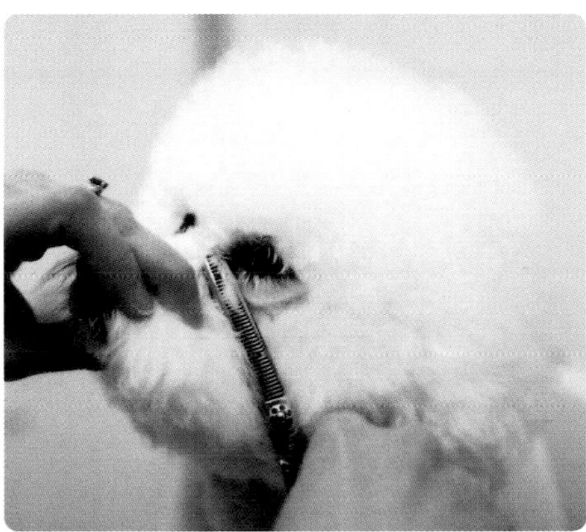

Again using your curved sheers trim away any hairs that stand out in front of the eyes and from the top of the muzzle.

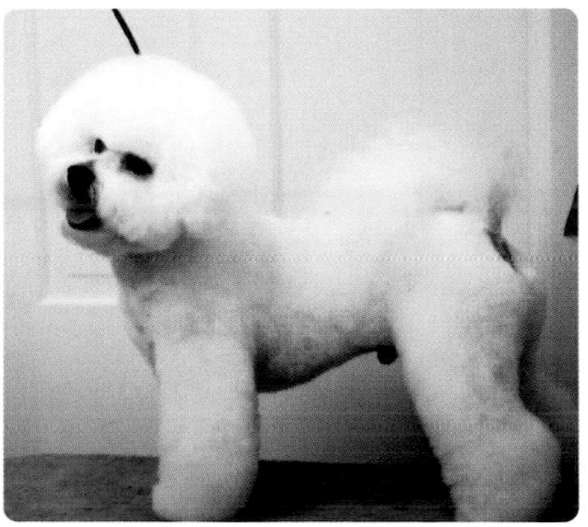

This photo shows the completed trim. Look at your Bichon and see where more hair has to be taken off to give the finished look.

Chapter Nine

Seniors

A Bichon Frise's first year of life is roughly equivalent to the first 15 years of a person's life. While some dogs, like toy breeds and terriers, live much longer lives than many working dogs like Great Danes and Boxers, canine–human age equivalency is the same for all breeds. Unlike humans, after a dog's first 12 months of life he is an adolescent. After that five or six years of human life is equal to one year of a dog's life. In other words, at seven years of age your Bichon is equivalent to a human of roughly 45–50 years old. A dog that lives to 17 is like a person living to be 100.

The Bichon Frise has an excellent life expectancy. It is not at all unusual for many of them to live well into their teens. Some Bichons live out their lives in a healthy, vigorous condition so it is difficult to state when your Bichon will begin to exhibit aging symptoms. At any rate, at this stage Pierre may have become pretty set in his ways and hopefully these are wise and reliable.

The old timer may be a bit crotchety at times and not too inclined to put up with inconsiderate puppies and children. Activity slows down considerably and he may experience the common symptoms of old age: arthritis, digestive difficulties, and bowel and bladder retention issues.

Just because Pierre has reached those twilight years doesn't mean he has to stop living! The older fellow will still enjoy taking walks with you every day. Maybe Pierre won't be thrilled about heading outdoors on cold or blustery days but when the weather is fair, there is absolutely no reason why the two of you can't be out there taking a nice leisurely walk around the block or down to the park. Don't push those walks to the limit and don't throw balls and Frisbees for too long a time—even though the old codger may think he's still capable of doing the 100-yard dash. Be kind and be careful with the old folks (human and canine) and they'll be with you for a long, long time.

To prepare for the eventual demise of the aging Bichon, some owners bring a puppy into the home. This is an understandable practice, but how it is done is extremely important. The old-timer has spent years earning his place of seniority, and suddenly he is faced with an exuberant and probably cuter intruder who draws the oohs and ahhs of visitors and the attention of his own people.

You can't blame the old fellow for feeling threatened or displaced when this happens. It is very important that the senior canine gets as much (more?) of the day's attention. He has earned it and deserves to be considered "King."

Senior Bichon Health Issues

Incontinence

After years of being perfectly housebroken you are distressed to find that Pierre has begun to urinate in the house. A bit of old age "leakage" is not entirely unusual, but on the other hand it could indicate an infection or loss of muscle tone. Your veterinarian can be of assistance in either case.

Tumors

Regular and thorough grooming is very important for the older Bichon. This is the time you should thoroughly check the skin all over the body. Seniors are prone to lumps and bumps that in most cases are benign tumors. Benign tumors are round and soft and do not seem to be strongly attached to the dog's skin. Nothing really has to be done about them, but in the event their size and shape change or change rapidly, bring them to the attention of your veterinarian. He may want to schedule their removal or a biopsy.

CAUTION

If you are in doubt about how to handle any health problem, telephone your veterinarian, who will know the questions to ask to determine whether it is necessary to bring your Bichon into the hospital or if there is an emergency procedure you should begin at once.

Stiffness

Arthritis is common in older dogs of nearly all breeds, including Bichons, but stiffness can also be the result of Pierre forgetting just how many years he's clocked and overdoing it a bit. Cold and damp weather can exacerbate the condition, especially in the morning. Keeping your old fellow trim in the weight department and appropriately active can help considerably. While there is no cure for arthritis your veterinarian can prescribe anti-inflammatory medications and food supplements that will make life more comfortable for your senior Bichon.

Deafness and Blindness

Deaf and blind dogs can get on surprisingly well. Sight is not a dog's primary sense to begin with—smell is. Owners are amazed how easily the blind dog learns to maneuver a household. Bumping into things is a rare occurence as long as furniture is not constantly being moved from one place to another. Deafness and blindness can easily be detected by your veterinarian and in some instances he can recommend surgery to assist vision. Cataracts can be treated with medications and surgery.

Dogs with these handicaps should never be allowed off leash when away from their home. They can't see approaching hazards and are not able to hear your warnings.

Diet

Reduced calorie senior diets are available in both dry and moist forms but since most Bichons retain all their teeth well into old age I strongly advise keeping your old fellow on kibble if that is what he is used to eating and your veterinarian hasn't recommended otherwise. Kibble will help to keep Pierre's teeth in good condition. Large knucklebones and chew toys are good in that respect as well.

Keep the old fellow well groomed and be sure his bed is in a warm, dry corner of the house through the winter months. He will appreciate that very much.

Eating properly and maintaining a sensible exercise program will keep you both happier and healthier a lot longer, but it is up to you to design the menus and implement the exercise program. Pierre will be happy to help but he won't be able to get you into your walking shoes, nor can he cook.

The Inevitable "Last Day"

Eventually, regardless of how well you care for the old fellow, Pierre will reach his last day with you. He may choose a day to lie down on his favorite napping spot and not wake up. The decision has been made. However, it is not always that easy.

Just as often it will be up to the owner to make the inevitable decision as to what will be Pierre's last day on earth. There is no hard and fast rule concerning this decision. It differs for every dog and every owner who will be forced to face the reality of that day.

Owners themselves know how healthy their old dog is in a way that no outside source can really advise. It will be up to the owner, weighing the veterinarian's advice against how well the old timer is doing, to decide just when the final day will be.

Veterinarians I have known are disinclined to *tell* the owner whether the day has arrived or not and do their best to leave the time for the final day up to the owner. They are not being evasive, only following medical ethics and guidelines. Owners are able to read between the lines, however, and without really wanting to be told what to do are intelligent enough to know when all sensible precautions and measures have been taken.

Euthanasia and Burial

The process of having a beloved pet put to sleep, although distressing for the owner, is not painful to the pet. The dog does not suffer; he simply goes to sleep. The decision to be at your Bichon's side when he is euthanized is purely personal and there is no real "answer." For some, being present makes the decision easier; for others, it is more upsetting than they are able to handle.

As if the loss of a beloved pet isn't enough to deal with, owners must decide what to do with the remains afterward. There are pet cemeteries that offer services as complete as an owner might want to obtain.

Many veterinary hospitals maintain crematoria or have arrangements with one where owners can have their pet cremated and obtain the ashes. The ashes can be kept in an urn or scattered in a place the dog especially liked. A dog I once owned was happiest when we at the beach together, so I took his ashes there and while thinking of the many fun days we had spent along the coast, I released his ashes to the winds so that he could remain there for all time to come. It provided a great feeling of release for me.

The Days After

The loss of a long-time canine friend and companion creates a void not easy to fill. Everything in the owner's home will serve as a reminder of the little fellow who is no longer there. Most owners I know who have lost their beloved Bichons feel it helps to remove as many reminders as possible, giving away things like favorite toys, leashes, and feeding and water bowls. Removing sad reminders does help alleviate the pain of loss at least to some degree.

Those who have lived alone with their pet may well experience the loss even more deeply than those who reside with other family members or friends. The death of their pet can seem as if "everything is gone." It is only natural to grieve, and for the person whose dog was their best or only friend, the grieving process will seldom be an easy one.

The answer to the problem that most friends give is simply, "Get another dog." Easier said than done for many. That said, there is no "right" time to get another dog. It may be at once or it may take many months to get to the place where the grieving person is ready to embark on an entirely new relationship with man's best friend.

Chapter Ten

Special Considerations

Exercise is something your Bichon needs and it will also improve your health and state of mind. You don't have to be fit for a marathon to give your Bichon much needed exercise. Good old-fashioned walking at a sensible pace is good for both you and the dog. Even better, exercise is a great mood neutralizer for both you and your dog.

Walking and Hiking

One of the special joys of owning a Bichon Frise is that, though their compact size accommodates a small apartment (or sports car), the breed is hardy enough to enjoy a good, long hike in the country. Your Bichon will enjoy the health benefits of exploring the countryside as much as you do.

Be sure to bring the proper equipment with you on your hikes. Stash any emergency and first aid materials that might be appropriate to the time of the year and the terrain. Park rangers and the Department of Parks and Recreation can advise you on what you should carry in case of emergency.

Hiking supplies for both dog and dog owner are available at specialty shops and through catalogs. Hiking with dogs has become so popular that a wide range of equipment is geared to the canine set alone. Collapsible food and drink containers, booties to protect your dog's feet from sharp rocks or freezing terrain, and rainwear.

Most national parks allow dogs but enforce very strict leash laws to protect the wildlife. Your Pierre may be small but he has no less a desire to catch that little critter that scampers by than some of the bigger fellows. And don't forget Pierre is a hairy dog—a brush and a comb are an absolute *must!*

Safety Issues

Your veterinarian will also be able to advise you on any special precautions you may have to take depending upon the area to which you are traveling. The risk of contracting tick-borne Lyme disease and heartworm increase in certain parts of the country.

CAUTION

If you are traveling any distance be aware that most states throughout the country, as well as Canada and Mexico, will require up-to-date vaccination against rabies. Crossing the border to Canada and Mexico will also require health certificates validated by your veterinarian. Be sure your rabies inoculations are current and that your Bichon is wearing the tag issued by your veterinarian.

A collar with identification tags is an excellent way for someone to put you and your Bichon back together if you somehow become separated. But what if the collar comes loose? Tracing you then becomes impossible.

There are other ways to ID your dog, of course. Tattooing, with your driver's license number or another traceable number, like a registry number from the American, Canadian, or United Kennel Clubs has been popular for years.

A surefire method of positive identification that cannot become separated from your dog is the microchip. It is about the size of a grain of rice and has an unalterable code on it that can be easily read by a scanner. Your veterinarian can insert the chip under the dog's skin between the shoulders with a syringe.

After the microchip has been inserted, the animal can be registered with the AKC Companion Animal Recovery program for a one-time fee that enrolls the animal for life. When your lost pet is turned in to an animal shelter or veterinarian, they will to scan the animal to see if he is carrying a chip. Scanners have become standard equipment in most shelters and veterinary offices around the country and the microchips have proven harmless to the animals carrying them.

Schering-Plough Animal Health distributes the microchip under the name "Home Again" and the AKC provides the database management services for a national recovery program. Your own veterinarian can give you more information about "Home Again" or you can contact the organization directly at (888) 466-3242. AKC Companion Animal Recovery can provide information as well by phone at (800) 252-7984 or by fax at (919) 233-1290. You can also visit their web site at *www.akccar.org*

Vacations

Your Bichon is a part of the family whether the family is just the two of you or a whole brood. So why shouldn't Pierre share in the fun you will be having on your vacation? If you've done your job well and Pierre is well trained and well socialized, reap some of the rewards of all your effort and bring him along.

Your Bichon will enjoy his adventures and can make the experience enjoyable for you. Take a tip from the singles crowd and think of your Bichon as an "ice breaker." You will be amazed by how many people find it much easier to strike up a conversation with you when they can start with comments

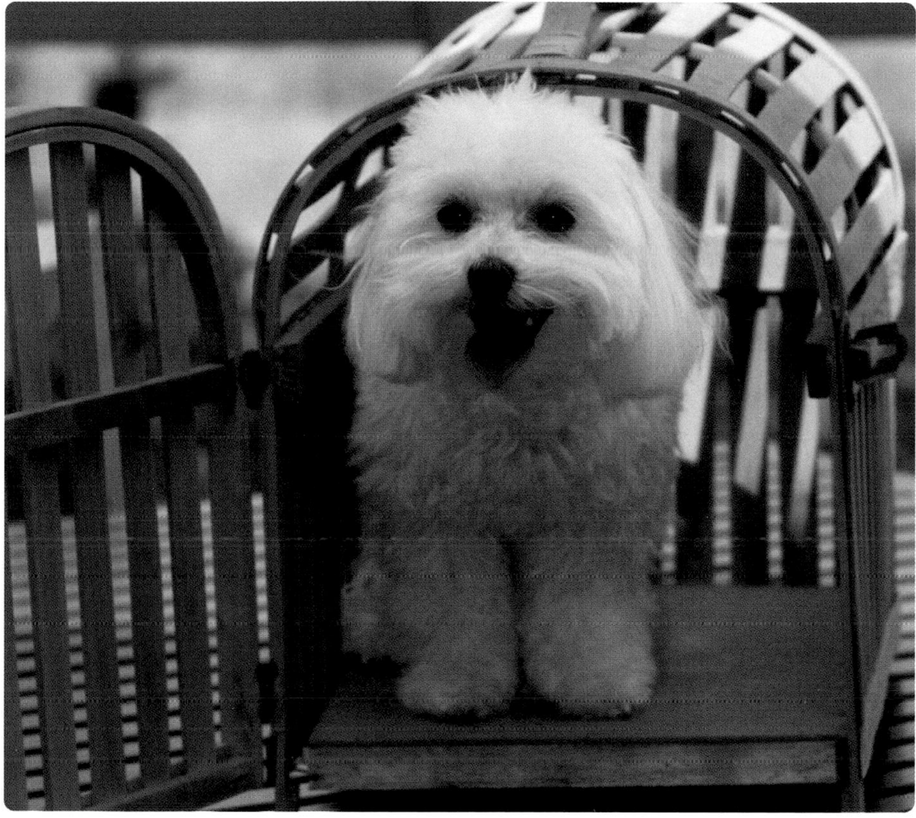

on your pooch. (I have several young male friends who borrow dogs to take to our local dog park with a great deal more in mind than dog walking!)

Your Bichon can also provide protection. Those with less than honorable intentions are inclined to shy away from a child or family being watched over by a dog of any size. You can always feel confident that your auto alarm is engaged when your Bichon is standing by.

Lakeside cottages and mountain cabins provide a degree of privacy and plenty of opportunity for family fun and social events in nearby towns. A good friend of ours spends a couple of weeks each year on a houseboat with wife, daughter, and the family Bichon. A hiking–camping trip provides lots of fun and adventure, to say nothing of the excellent exercise in the great outdoors.

Finding Dog-Friendly Lodging

Not all hotels and motels accept dogs. You may not be the type of person who likes to have structured travel plans, but reserving dog-friendly lodging before you begin your journey is the smart thing to do. Driving until you are totally exhausted and then starting a search for dog-friendly accommodations is not an attractive option.

Speak directly to hotel or motel personnel beforehand. Even though some establishments advertise the fact that they accept dogs, this may be resticted to certain small dogs or dogs may be required to be confined outside the rooms in their own travel crates.

Helpful Hints

Each year the Automobile Association of America (AAA) puts out updated catalogs listing dog-friendly accommodations by city and state. Dawbert Press publishes a series of dog-friendly travel guides written by Dawn and Robert Habgood called *On the Road Again with Man's Best Friend*. Each is devoted to specific geographic areas of the country.

Car Travel

Before you embark on any kind of trip, whether it's down to the shopping mall or across the state, there are a number of things you must think seriously about. Two of the most important are temperature and the length of time required for the stops you will be making. Traveling in an air-conditioned car or van won't affect your dog adversely—if you don't plan to stop.

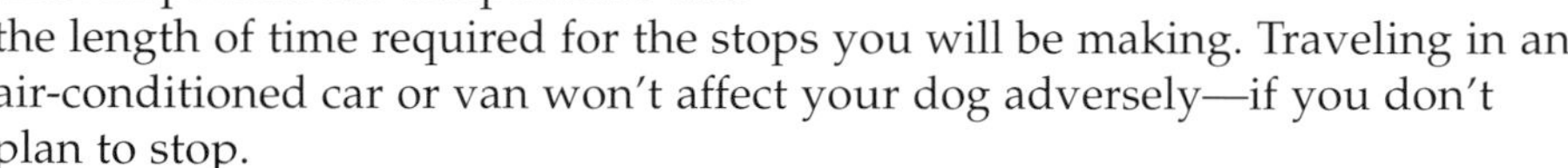

Although temperatures in the low 80s don't impress us as being unusually hot, temperatures inside a car, even with open windows, can soar into the 100s in less time than it takes you to run in and out of a service station for a rest stop. Your dog can sustain permanent brain damage or death at these temperatures.

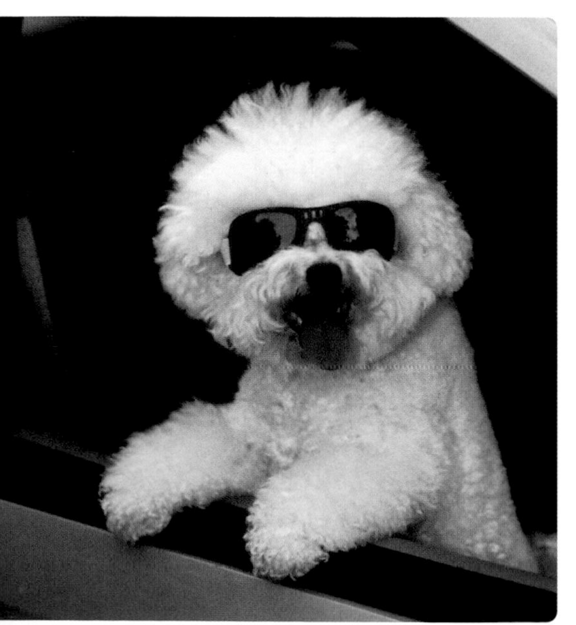

Do not take chances! Your stops and dining choices may have to be restricted to drive-throughs so that you can keep the air-conditioning going.

Safety

The safest place for your Bichon when a car is in motion is safely enclosed in his shipping kennel or crate. Sudden stops can throw your dog against dividers or a window and cause severe injury or death.

Whether with doggy seat belts or in a crate, all dogs should be restrained for safety's sake. Travel crates also provide a safe place to keep your dog when the two of you arrive at your destination. Your host or the hotel at which you will be staying may not approve of your treasured pal parading around loose night and day.

Traveling by Air

If your plans include traveling by air, the whole picture becomes a bit more complicated. Not impossible mind you, but certainly not as easy as having your Bichon safely secured in his travel cage in the back of your van.

Bichons can be carried on board in a specially designed pet travel case that will fit under the seat in front of you. Pets cannot be taken out of the travel cases while you travel.

CAUTION

When your Bichon arrives at his destination he will undoubtedly be ecstatic to see you or the person who is picking him up. Do not take him out of his crate until you are in a secure area and snap a leash on his collar *before* he steps out of the crate. Airline terminals can be hectic and if your dog slips away you could have a terrible time trying to catch him.

TRAVEL CHECKLIST

Night before

✔ **Freeze water.** Fill one of the shipping crate's water bowls and put it in your freezer the night before you ship your Bichon. Just before you leave home take the frozen cup out of the freezer and place it in the crate. This will melt gradually and provide water for your Bichon for a longer period of time and with less spillage.

✔ **Call the airline.** Find out exactly where and at what time your dog should arrive at the airport. Most airlines will take your dog at the check-in counter if he is traveling as excess baggage. If you are shipping your dog ahead, you may have to go to the airline's freight office.

The day you ship

✔ **Prepare the shipping crate according to regulations.** You must line the bottom of the crate with absorbent bedding. Food and water in dishes that are attached to the inside of the crate's wire door are also required. Tape a small bag of food to the top of the crate along with food and water instructions for the next 24 hours in case of delays. Crates cannot be locked but may be double fastened with bungee cords for added safety.

✔ **Tape a "live animal" sticker on the crate.** Airlines have these stickers available at point of departure. Also tape a sign giving full information regarding contact persons at both ends of the trip along with the necessary phone numbers. Cell phones do have their time and place and this is one of them. You or the receiving party must be able to be reached without delay.

✔ **Make sure your dog wears a collar with I.D. tags.** Accidents do happen and dogs have been known to escape from their crates. If your Bichon should elude officials and get beyond the airport premises there will be no way for anyone to contact you unless the dog carries identification.

BE PREPARED! Bichons on the Go

Whether your Bichon is traveling in cargo as excess baggage or being shipped on ahead, there are a good number of safety measures that will help increase the odds of his safe arrival at the other end:

1. **Contact the airlines.** Call the airlines you prefer and check out all their policies regarding shipping dogs. Your final decision should go to the airline that promises the greatest safety for your dog.
2. **Understand the rules.** Airlines have many have rules and regulations about the kind and sizes of shipping kennels they'll accept, how the dog should be identified, and what kind of health and inoculation regulations apply.
3. **Reconfirm reservations.** Confirm your dog's reservation before the actual departure date of the flight.
4. **Choose direct, nonstop flights when possible.** Opt for early morning direct flights especially during warm weather months. Avoid flights that have connections along the way, especially if those connections mean a change of airlines.
5. **Bring health certificates.** Your dog should travel with a current health certificate signed by your veterinarian. Even though the airline might not require one for shipping, the office at the receiving end may require a health certificate to unload your dog. Discuss travel plans with your veterinarian. Some veterinarians discourage shipping very young or geriatric dogs and strongly advise against shipping females that are in an advanced stage of pregnancy.
6. **Avoid sedatives and tranquilizers.** Dogs accustomed to spending time in their travel kennels usually settle down once they are loaded onto the plane and sleep the entire flight. Avoid using sedatives and tranquilizers unless absolutely necessary. In most cases they are more appropriate for the owner who is traveling than they are for the dog.
7. **Use an airline approved shipping kennel.** Buying your shipping kennel directly from the airline on which you are shipping your dog will ensure there's no last-minute problem with approvals. If you do bring your own crate, the airline will insist that the kennel be large enough for your dog to stand up and turn around in. *You* must insist that it be no larger than that. The travel crate is not meant to be a playground. Those that are too roomy run the risk of your dog being thrown from side to side in turbulent weather.

There is a charge for carrying a pet on board. Each airline sets its own price structure for this service.

If your Bichon is not going to travel in the cabin, he must fly as excess baggage in the cargo hold of the plane. Here again the charge for this service increases steadily with each passing year so it will be necessary to inquire about the cost when making your own reservation. At that time you must make a reservation for your dog as well. Airlines limit the number of pets

that can be carried on any one flight. Also note that federal regulations require that no animal be shipped by air if the ground temperature at either end of the flight is above 85 degrees or below 45 degrees.

Boarding Kennels and Pet Sitters

If traveling with Pierre seems impractical, you just may decide that the best vacation for the two of you is one spent apart—you at a deluxe resort in the Bahamas and Pierre at a delightful doggy dude ranch. There are some really wonderful boarding kennels that will take super care of your pal while you're gone.

Think it's impossible to find anyone who will care for Pierre like you do? That may be true, but there is a kennel out there that will do a very adequate job in your absence. One of my dogs is mad for the kennel where he "vacations" while I'm away. All I need to say is "doggie dude ranch?" and he's at the door!

Finding a good kennel will take a little research. Ask your vet for kennel recommendations or contact the American Boarding Kennel Association. Your breeder and your neighbors are also good sources of information.

Even with recommendations, no kennel is adequate for your Bichon unless it meets *your* approval. When you have several kennels that sound interesting, drop by during business hours and ask for a tour. Understand that few kennels are going to be as neat and spiffy as your kitchen or living room—imagine your own home with a couple of dozen dogs in it. This doesn't mean, however, that the kennel should show signs of unsanitary conditions and neglect. It's hard to keep any kennel smelling sweeter than cherry blossoms in springtime, but bad smells and smells that hang through the air no matter where you go don't offer much promise of sanitary conditions.

If your Bichon wants and needs attention, make sure the kennel attendants will be able to provide it. Many kennels offer "playtime," a romp in a large paddock and someone to play catch with. They may charge a few dollars per day more for this service but it can mean a big difference in Pierre's stay.

Find out what experience the prospective sitter has had with small dogs and Bichons specifically. A good sitter should have a good sense of how smaller dogs should be dealt with.

All responsible boarding kennels have health precautions and inoculation requirements. Be sure to find out what these are and how long before your dog arrives the inoculations must be given. If your dog has the entire required inoculations, ask how long the kennel finds them valid. Good kennels demand proof of current rabies inoculations and protection against kennel cough. Many ask what precautions you are using against fleas and ticks. If none of these precautions are in place—*go elsewhere!*

When you check your pal in be sure to leave your veterinarian's name, address, and phone number in case of emergency and do leave a contact number where you can be reached quickly while you're gone. If Pierre is on a special diet of any kind be sure to take a more than adequate supply of that food with you when you check him in.

Pet Sitters

If you are not comfortable leaving your dog in a kennel consider a pet sitter.

A pet sitter is someone who will either stay in your home or visit daily at regular intervals during the day while you are gone. Pet sitters not only feed stay-at-home dogs but play with them and take them out for walks.

Just about everyone has a good friend who is willing to do these pet sitting chores with your Bichon for a day or two. Longer than a few days becomes an imposition. Paying a professional sitter may be the smarter thing to do. Your veterinarian may be able to recommend someone and

there are national organizations dedicated to making recommendations for qualified pet sitters.

Do understand that anyone can advertise himself or herself as a "professional." Professional pet sitters who are members of a national organization such as the National Association of Professional Pet Sitters (NAPPS) are usually bonded and insured. They have identification that can be verified as to their membership and standing. Their organization can provide you with references.

When you believe you have found the right sitter, check to see if that individual has had experience with Bichons (or at least small dogs). Make sure that everything in the sitter's agreement covers the items you believe are important. The sitter should provide you with a list of questions concerning what he needs to know about your dog and your home.

Make certain that you and the sitter will be able to reach each other in case of emergency. Exchange 24-hour contact information and make sure that the person is familiar with the laws or area rules and regulations that govern animal care in your area: leash laws, barking dogs, etc.

The two of you should be absolutely clear on the charges for the service and what is done in your absence. You don't want to anticipate a bill for a few hundred dollars and find out on your return that it is actually in the thousands!

Resources

This chapter provides of a list of the media all Bichon Frise owners may have use for in their day-to-day lives with their treasured companions. Books and magazines, videos, Web sites, and trade organizations abound, ready to help you along in just about any pursuit you wish to follow with your Bichon.

Kennel Clubs

American Kennel Club
51 Madison Avenue
New York, NY 10010
(212) 696-8200
Registration Information
American Kennel Club
5580 Centerview Drive
Raleigh, NC 27606
(919) 233-9767
www.akc.org

American Temperament Test Society, Inc.
P.O. Box 800130
Balch Springs, TX 75180
(972) 557-2887
www.atts.org

Bichon Frise Club of America
140 Pine Avenue
Clarksburg, MA 01247-4602
(413) 663-7109
www.bichon.org

Canadian Kennel Club
89 Skyway Avenue, Unit 100
Etobicoke, Ontario
Canada M9W 6R4
(416) 675-5511
www.ckc.ca/info

United Kennel Club
100 E. Kilgore Road
Kalamazoo, Michigan 49001-5598
(269) 343-9020
www.ukcdogs.com

Periodicals

AKC Gazette
51 Madison Avenue
New York, New York 10010
(800) 533-7323
www.akc.org

Bichon Frise Reporter
P.O. Box 6369
San Luis Obispo, CA 93412
(805) 528-2007
www.bichonfrisereporter.com

Bloodlines Magazine
United Kennel Club
100 E. Kilgore Road
Kalamazoo, Michigan 49001-5598
www.ukcdogs.com

Dog Fancy
P.O. Box 6050
Mission Viejo, CA 92690
(800) 426-2516
www.dogfancy.magazine.com

Dog World
P.O. Box 6050
Mission Viejo, CA 92690
(800) 426-2516
www.dogworldmag.com

Dogs in Canada
Apex Publishers
89 Skyway Avenue, #200
Etobicoke, Ontario, Canada
M9W-6R4
www.dogsincanada.com

Dogs in Review
P.O. Box 6050
Mission Viejo, CA 92690
(800) 426-2516
www.dogchannel.com

Journal of Veterinary Medical Education
Association of Veterinary Medical Colleges (AVMC)
1101 Vermont Ave., NW #301
Washington, DC 20005
www.jvmeonline.org

Books

Beauchamp, Richard G. *Bichon Frise: A Complete Pet Owner's Manual.* Hauppauge, New York: Barron's Educational Series, Inc., 1996.

———. *Solving the Mysteries of Breed Type.* Freehold, New Jersey: Kennel Club Books, 2008.

Colflesh, Linda. *Making Friends (Training Your Dog Positively).* New York, New York: Howell Book House, 1990.

Squire, Dr. Ann. *Understanding Man's Best Friend.* New York, New York: Macmillan Publishing Company, 1991.

Stubbs, Barbara. *The Complete Bichon Frise.* New York, New York: Howell Book House, 1990.

Pet Travel Publications

The Automobile Association of America (AAA)
(800) 222-4357
www.aaa.com

On the Road Again with Man's Best Friend
Dawbert Press
order@dawbert.com

Vacationing with Your Pet Guide
Pet-Friendly Publications
2327 Ward Road
Pocomoke City, MD 28851

Pet Travel Resources from Air Safe.com
www.airsafe.com/issues/pets.htm

Boarding Kennels and Pet Sitters

Pet Care Services Association
(Formerly American Boarding Kennels Association)
1702 East Pikes Peak Avenue
Colorado Springs, CO 80909
(877) 570-7788
www.petcareservices.org

National Association of Professional Pet Sitters
15000 Commerce Parkway, Suite C
Mt. Laurel, NJ 08054
(856) 439-0324
www.petsitters.org

Pet Sitters International
418 East King Street
King, NC 27021
Phone: (336) 983-9222
www.petsit.com

Videos

AKC and the Sport of Dogs
American Kennel Club

Right Dog for You
American Kennel Club

Breed Standard Videos
American Kennel Club

Health

American Veterinary Medical Association
1931 North Meacham Road, Suite 100
Schaumburg, IL 60173-4360
Phone: (847) 925-8070
Fax: (847) 925-1329
E-mail: avmainfo@avma.org
www.avma.org

Rescue

Bichon Frise Rescue
www.bichon.resq.org

National Animal Poison Control Center
(800) 548-2423
www.napcc.aspca.org

Identification Organizations

American Kennel Club Home Again Microchip Program
8051 Arco Corporate Drive, Suite 200
Raleigh, NC 27617-3900
(800) 252-7984

Int. American Veterinary Identification Systems, Inc.
3179 Hammer Avenue
Norco, CA 92860
(800) 336-AVID
www.avidid.com

Sports and Games

North American Flyball Association, Inc.
1400 West Devon Avenue, #512
Chicago, IL 60660
(800) 318-6312
www.flyball.org

U.S. Dog Agility Association, Inc.
300 South Kirby Street, Suite 101
Garland, TX 75042-7433
(972) 487-2200
www.usdaa.com

Alpo Canine Frisbee Disc Championships
www.alpo.com

Therapy Dog Organizations

Therapy Dogs International, Inc.
88 Bartley Road
Flanders, NJ 07836
(973) 252-9800
www.tdi-dog.org

Delta Society
875-124th Avenue NE
Bellevue, WA 98005
(425) 679-5500
www.deltasociety.org

Index

THE TEAM BEHIND THE *TRAIN YOUR DOG* DVD

Host **Nicole Wilde** is a certified Pet Dog Trainer and internationally recognized author and lecturer. Her books include *So You Want to be a Dog Trainer* and *Help for Your Fearful Dog* (Phantom Publishing). In addition to working with dogs, Nicole has been working with wolves and wolf hybrids for over fifteen years and is considered an expert in the field.

Host **Laura Bourhenne** is a Professional Member of the Association of Pet Dog Trainers, and holds a degree in Exotic Animal Training. She has trained many species of animals including several species of primates, birds of prey, and many more. Laura is striving to enrich the lives of pets by training and educating the people they live with.

Director **Leo Zahn** is an award winning director/cinematographer/editor of television commercials, movies, and documentaries. He has directed and edited more than a dozen instructional DVDs through the Picture Company, a subsidiary of Picture Palace, Inc., based in Los Angeles.